Advance Praise for Power Up for Profits!

Kathleen has written THE definitive online marketing manifesto for women. And although this powerhouse of a book is filled with proven strategies, tactics and concrete practical steps, it's Kathleen's seasoned, take charge, no-nonsense presence that is the most valuable part of this book... her steady and generous hand guides the reader toward stepping into all she can be... as a businesswoman and as a person.

Every woman online entrepreneur, beginner or seasoned professional, should read this book. Kathleen's wisdom will not only help you succeed in the online world; her sage advice, stories and deep insights into business and human nature will help every woman exert a positive influence on her company, her customers and on her community.

—Dr. Ellen Britt, PA, Ed.D.
Marketing Qi
http://www.marketingqi.com

If you want to turn your message into your business – get this book. If your message already is your business and you want to make it bigger, monetize it better, and impact more people – get this book! The hypnotic blend of stories, examples, specific, immediately usable advice and how-to tips make this book something much better than just a marketing guide; it's a step-by-step blueprint about how to power up your life and turn your passions into a profitable business.

—Adam Urbanski
Marketing Mentors Inc.
http://themarketingmentors.com

Kathleen Gage has hit this one out of the park with her book *Power Up for Profits!* I love her straight forward approach of telling you exactly what it takes to have a successful online business. Nothing is sugar coated with Kathleen, and that is exactly what you need to succeed! It's a quick, fast and fun read, while teaching you online marketing at the same time. Her passion to help you comes through, and is inspiring.

—Christina Hills
Website Creation Workshop
http://www.websitecreationworkshop.com

With wit and wisdom, Kathleen Gage shares her years of experience in a practical way. Readers will be able to immediately power up their profits by implementing her advice in their businesses. This is a must-read for anyone who's serious about generating consistent revenue online.

—Marnie Pehrson
Ignite Point
http://www.ignitepoint.com/

Definitely a must-read book for anyone serious about achieving the dream of building a successful online business! Kathleen Gage has the unique ability to take you by the hand and show you how abundant business success can be created. In addition to blowing away all of the myths you've been taught about spiritually focused entrepreneurship, she cuts through the hype and gets down to the nitty-gritty of showing you how to turn your passions into profits!

—Nancy Marmolejo
Nancita Inc. / TalentAndGenius.com
http://talentandgenius.com

If you're struggling with the changing paradigm of business and making money, this book is for you! Within these pages, Kathleen Gage provides powerful advice that is strategic, systematic, synergistic – all of this, in a spiritually-focused way. The result is that you'll be able to develop an online business that really works for YOU and those you're here to serve. What a gem!

—Christine Kloser
Christine Kloser Companies LLC
www.christinekloser.com

Kathleen Gage is one of a rare breed of entrepreneurs who thinks of others before themselves. Her knowledge runs deep, her instincts are uncanny, and her wit is delightful. If you have the opportunity to connect with Kathleen, I urge you to make the most of it. Allow her inside of your head, your heart, and your business and she will help you to move towards a life you may have never before imagined.

—Connie Ragen Green
Small Business Unmarketing
http://connieragengreen.com

Kathleen Gage's *Power Up for Profits!* is a tour de force of the savvy and cutting edge marketing acumen that every business needs combined with those all important elements of "Heart" and "Service" that are at the core of every truly great business. Get this book now. Read it. Profit from it!

—Daniel Hall
Daniel Hall Combined Enterprises
www.DanielHallPresents.com

There are great books on spiritual principles to co-create the circumstances of our dreams. There are even more books on business development and the management of those dreams. But one of the things I've noticed when talking to Kathleen is that she doesn't separate the two. Finally, someone – Kathleen Gage – is bringing both dimensions into an inspirational how-to book that not only improves your business a hundredfold, but also makes sure every minute of doing it is serving the greater good. What a joy!

—David Perdew
Niche Affiliate Marketing System, Inc.
https://mynams.com/

Kathleen Gage walks her talk. *Power Up for Profits!* reveals the exact strategies and tactics I watched Kathleen use to build her successful business for the 7 years I've known and worked with her. Everything she teaches she has tested and proven successful or you wouldn't be reading about it. Read the book, then implement. With Kathleen's guidance, you have the power to be successful too.

—Denise Wakeman
The Blog Squad LLC
http://DeniseWakeman

If you thought you knew everything about how to be successful in business, wait until you read what's inside *Power Up for Profits!* Having grown from homeless at 25 to fantastically successful entrepreneur today, Kathleen combines insightful stories with specific to-dos to teach anyone how to achieve business success doing what they love to do in a spiritually oriented fashion!

—Don Crowther
Don Crowther
http://doncrowther.com/

In *Power Up for Profits!*, Kathleen Gage draws on her extensive knowledge and nearly two decades of experience in online marketing to provide entrepreneurs with a road map for success. This powerful guide will equip you with time-tested strategies that will allow you to develop your own profitable, online business.

Discover how to clearly identify your target audience so you can reach the exact people who are hungry for your message. Accelerate your success by getting your copy of this gem today. Kathleen Gage, a woman of great knowledge and integrity, has clearly paved the way for you to power up and profit!

—Dvorah Lansky
Digital Publishing Cafe
http://www.digitalpublishingcafe.com

Woo hoo! Somebody has finally put all the critical pieces to dialing in marketing for business owners in one place, in a way that's easily digestible and aligned with attraction principles. This book is going straight on my resource webpage for all of my clients to devour. Right on, Kathleen!

—Jeanna Gabellini
MasterPeace Coaching
www.masterpeacecoaching.com

Most entrepreneurs are running east, looking for a sunset. Kathleen Gage is the guide you need to ensure you arrive at your dream destination. Kathleen's new book *Power Up for Profits!* is the real deal and a must for anyone who wants to monetize their passion. It should be required reading for all entrepreneurs.

—Sam Crowley
Every Day Is Saturday
http://everydayissaturday.com/

In a world of ambiguity, Kathleen takes a sniper's approach to helping you aim directly for the bull's-eye. Understanding that doing "good" and doing "well" do not have to be mutually exclusive, Kathleen teaches you precisely what to do and HOW to do it while encouraging you to never apologize for earning what you're worth. Having witnessed Kathleen command the stage and captivate her audience, she absolutely walks the walk. Read this book and you too can live bold and profit!

—Steve Olsher
America's Reinvention Expert
www.steveolsher.com

No one offers wisdom on turning your passion into a profitable business like Kathleen Gage. *Power Up for Profits!* is her best book yet on online marketing wisdom. It provides an easy step-by-step guide to master this powerful arena and make your unique contribution to the world.

—Viki Winterton
Expert Insights Publishing
www.ExpertInsightsPublishing.com

Dare to read *Power up for Profits!* only if you're ready to roll up your shirt sleeves and get the straight scoop on what really works in business today! Addressing both the inner and outer game of marketing and business, Kathleen Gage brilliantly blends her from-the-trenches experience with proven results of her own and those of her clients. A no-nonsense primer on winning the entrepreneurial game that every woman business owner should read cover to cover – and over and over.

—Marcia Bench
Marcia Bench Enterprises, LLC
www.yourdivinegifts.com

As an experienced business and marketing strategist myself, I found myself continually nodding in agreement as I read Kathleen Gage's *Power Up for Profits!* She's honest and straightforward – something else I truly appreciate – and clearly focuses on why something works so women will have a keen understanding as marketing tactics grow, change or even disappear. This definitely is a must-have resource for any woman starting a business who wants to make profits fast.

—Shannon Cherry
http://shannoncherry.com

You can take the rest of your life and try to figure out how to achieve great business success. Or you can follow the proven and tested spiritual principles and online marketing methods found in Kathleen Gage's new book, *Power Up for Profits!* It's your choice, do it the hard way... or do it the smart way!

—Ryan Eliason
Social Entrepreneur Empowerment Network
www.socialentrepreneurempowerment.com

Take every word of Kathleen's advice to heart because it is 100% accurate. It's presented with a no-nonsense, right-to-the-point approach that is refreshing and totally reflects Kathleen's personal style. You'll love her simple stories and examples that drive home each point she makes. Don't skip ahead. Read it right from the beginning because it will provide you with a powerful system for building a profitable online lifestyle business.

—Janis Pettit
Small Business, Big Results
http://smallbusiness-bigresults.com

Power Up For Profits!

The Smart Woman's Guide to Online Marketing

by Kathleen Gage

THOMAS NOBLE BOOKS

Permissions Department,
Thomas Noble Books
427 N Tatnall Street #90946
Wilmington, DE 19801-2230

.THOMAS NOBLE
BOOKS

Library of Congress Control Number: 2013940877
ISBN 978-0-9892357-0-9
Printed in the United States of America

Cover Design: Sarah Barrie, www.Cyanotype.ca
Editing: Gwen Hoffnagle

Table of Contents

Dedication

It is with incredible gratitude I dedicate this book to my friend, partner, companion, confidant, soul mate and life traveler, Karen Noel. You make me continuously strive to be the best person I can be and courageously live my truth.

My deepest love and appreciation to my mother and father for your gentle whispers of love and encouragement from the heavens.

Acknowledgements

With deepest appreciation

This book would not be complete without expressing my deepest appreciation to the many people who made the process of writing, publishing and bringing this book to market an amazing experience. You made the journey memorably joyful.

To Marnie Perhson for lighting the spark that encouraged me to commit to sharing my knowledge and getting the book written. To my amazing team Jama St. John, Chantal Beaupre, Melanie Borowczyk, Kathleen Mull and Terry Loving who tirelessly supported my vision and continually went above and beyond. To Gwen Hoffnagle for your wonderful perspective and editing. You knew exactly how to tighten up my message and words in a masterful way. To Sarah for your great cover design and nerves of steel.

To my publisher, Lynne Klippel, for your guidance, encouragement and support. I appreciate you more than words can say.

To Nettie and Irene for your continued encouragement and excitement that always makes me smile. I feel your love.

And to my dear sister Lorraine Lawson. I love you so very much and am incredibly grateful that the years have brought us so close. Your encouragement has meant more than you will know.

And to everyone who invested in this book, I am unbelievably grateful for your choice to let me into your life.

And to God for giving me another day to live my truth, share my knowledge and do my life's work.

Introduction

Face reality as it is, not as it was or as you wish it to be.

—Jack Welch

I love business and I love teaching people how to turn their passions into profitable businesses.

I built my business on the premise that you can run a business based on spiritual principles while generating great revenue that affords you an abundant lifestyle. Although the material in this book is about the physical plane of business, it is also grounded in the spiritual side of business. You can grow a successful business that allows you to bless others in deep and extraordinary ways. Your mindset is the cornerstone of living a life that others only dream of. For years I knew this way of life was possible, but I couldn't quite get a handle on it. Through my willingness to keep moving forward, today I *know* it is possible to have a business that allows you to accomplish more than the work you do.

In my live presentations I have been known to say, "The world is in a world of hurt. If what you do even remotely heals the minds, bodies, spirits, finances and relationships of your tribe, you absolutely must do all you can to get your message out to market." I decided to write this book at this time in order to teach as many conscious entrepreneurs as possible how to get their message out to as many people as possible in order to shift the energy of the planet.

My life's work is helping others get their messages out about *their* life's work.

What you will learn in the pages of *Power Up for Profits* is to honor the gifts that are your passion and life's work and accept that it is okay to make money doing your life's work. You will learn about what it takes to get your message "out to market" in a big way in order to make a difference and how to promote what you are doing. The more effectively you do this, the easier it is to fulfill your purpose.

Although the information in *Power Up for Profits* is perfect for any conscious and socially responsible woman who has already started her business, been in business for any length of time, or plans to start a business, the information is perfect for consciously aware men as well. We will explore how to use the Internet to gain world-wide visibility and reach more of your community or, to use the latest buzzword, your tribe. Visibility allows you to reach more people with your message, resulting in greater impact and fulfilling your life's work.

Regardless of your market and message, if you are here to make the world a better place, this book is for you. It may be that you are here to help middle-aged women live a healthier, more fulfilled life. Maybe your purpose is to teach communication skills to parents of troubled children. Perhaps it's to raise awareness about issues of animal abuse. It might be to help conscious entrepreneurs build their businesses. Maybe you are meant to help socially conscious authors learn how to write their manuscripts. Opportunity to fulfill your life purpose is ever-present. Your job is to answer the calling and choose to act on it.

Far too many people waste time mulling over what they should or should not be doing, when anything you can do to make the world a better place is part of your life's work and purpose.

Now is the best time in history to answer your calling and spread your message around the world.

I am going to assume that your life's work and your business go hand in hand. Regardless of what stage your business has reached, do the following:
➳ Identify your market
➳ Identify your expertise
➳ Position your expert status
➳ Package your expertise
➳ Market and sell

The "what" to do is the easy part. Knowing *how* to do it is a completely different story. In *Power Up for Profits* you will learn both the what and the how.

There are many different types of businesses that can be built using online methods whether they be virtually positioned or brick-and-mortar businesses. I work with conscious entrepreneurs who are experts in specific areas and want to reach as many people and markets as they can with their message. It's one thing to be viewed as an expert, but the challenge today is to stand out from the crowd.

By the time you finish *Power up for Profits,* you will know exactly how to gain visibility, position your expert status, and reach your market. The more you do this the more you will generate revenue. The more revenue you generate, the more of your life's work you can do and the more you can contribute to causes you believe in. Here are some of the keys to the concepts you'll learn about in this book:

➻ **Mindset**

No matter what training you receive and what skills you develop, without the right mindset, all is for naught. It's easy to keep a positive attitude when things are going your way; the true test is when things are not going your way and you are able to stay the course in spite of this.

➻ **Visibility**

The more visible you are to your market, the more impact you can have. Only fear and lack of commitment can limit your potential visibility. You will learn specific ways to gain massive visibility through various online means including social media.

➻ **Living in the light**

To have the greatest impact you must be willing to move away from the shadows and stand tall and proud of who you are and what you are here to do. Let the light shine on your message! It's amazing how we lurk in our own shadows, waiting for someone to give us permission to live in our greatness. Well, today is that day. You have permission.

➤ **Standing in your power**

To have the greatest impact you must be able to "stand" in your power – "own" your power – instead of blending in. (Blending in is fine if you want to live in the status quo.)

➤ **Fulfilling your purpose through your business**

Many of us dwell in "someday" – someday I will take the risks I need to take; someday I will write the book; someday I will play bigger. But when you live in someday, you will never fulfill your purpose. Today is the day. There is no time to waste.

➤ **Knowing your worth**

A huge part of fulfilling your purpose is knowing your worth. Many of us were told as youngsters to be quiet and keep our opinions to ourselves. You can no longer *afford* to do this, either literally or in regard to fulfilling your life purpose.

➤ **Developing short-term and long-term strategies**

To achieve the most in your business, thus the greatest impact in the world, short-term and long-term plans are essential. Don't fly by the seat of your pants; take the time to envision what you want, need, and desire. In *Power up for Profits* you will discover how to put your strategy in place, implement it, and gain the greatest results possible.

➤ **Gaining trust in the market**

The more your market knows you, the better. I call this the "know-like-trust factor." It takes time, effort, and commitment. There are a number of ways to build trust. Internet resources can help you build trust with your tribe in a very cost-effective way. The playing field has been leveled. What used to be reserved for the "big boys" is now available to virtually anyone who has a computer and online access.

➤ **Packaging your knowledge**

The best way to build your business and send your message out to the world is to package your knowledge into various types of information products. You and your tribe will benefit greatly when you offer your products and/or services using various "price points" – everything from free to products or programs that sell for tens of thousands of dollars. (For the sake of brevity I will use the word *product* throughout this book to refer to either a product or a service, unless otherwise noted.)

➻ **Being proactive**

Take the initiative to use the simple yet very powerful ways to get your message out to the world that you will find in *Power Up for Profits*. I am confident it *will* improve the lives of those you connect with.

When I began my business in 1994, I struggled with my business identity. The more ambiguous I was, the more I struggled to grow my business. I worked primarily with corporate and government entities. I had worked for GTE Health Systems, so it was a natural shift to move from working *for* a corporation to working *with* corporations. I classified myself as a corporate trainer in management, leadership, customer service, team building, etc. I was fortunate to secure a contract with a seminar company within a few months of starting my business. This gave me the breathing room to cultivate my business identity.

Once I figured out who I truly was, my purpose for being in business, and who I most desired to work with, everything changed. I love working with conscious and socially aware speakers, authors, consultants, artists, and other creative experts who want to get their messages out.

Imagine what life could be like if you were able to do the same. There is no reason you can't.

Let's get started!

Kathleen Gage,
Pleasant Hill, Oregon
July 2013

Chapter 1

Your Business is Your Expression

I have found that there are three types of entrepreneurs:

→ Those who dream of running a business but never do anything about it.

→ Those who start a business but try to do everything on a shoestring and never achieve their potential.

→ Those who embrace their role and responsibilities and do what it takes to get their message out to market.

You have been given the desire to impact others in a positive way for a reason, so don't let your fears stop you from being who you are meant to be, impacting those you are meant to impact, and realizing how important your role in business truly is.

It has been said, "Knowledge is power." This is *not* true. It's what we *do* with our knowledge that makes the difference. When you know how to position your expert status, gain visibility, and promote your business in a way that matches your highest values, you can literally write your own ticket to success and power.

In August of 2009 my business and my life were going great. I loved what I did, knew I was making a difference to thousands of men and women around the globe, and saw no end in sight. Like any business owner, I had my ups and downs, but with over fifteen years under my business belt, there were more ups than ever before.

I turned fifty-five, and decided to fulfill a longtime dream – to participate in a marathon. I began the training with every intention of participating in the Portland Marathon in October of that year. Then all hell broke loose. In the third month, after eight miles of training, I hit a pothole and snapped my ankle.

My greatest disappointment was that my mom and dad had planned on attending the marathon for my dad's eighty-second birthday. But soon after I broke my ankle, my dad was diagnosed with brain and lung cancer. Within four weeks he had passed away.

I couldn't even begin to understand what my mother was feeling. They had been married nearly sixty-one years, and she seemed so lost. She and my father were inseparable and did almost everything together.

Within days of my father's passing, my mom was rushed to the hospital for emergency surgery to remove over a foot and a half of her colon. And within a matter of two months I went from feeling like I had life by the tail to feeling like life was spinning out of control. Though I didn't know what would happen from day to day, I did know that my focus was drastically changing. I went from being extremely focused on my business to knowing that my primary purpose was to care for my mother. I had no idea how long I would be in this role; I just knew in my heart of hearts that this was where my focus needed to be.

This was the catalyst for me to become a product-creation maven. Although I had created some outstanding information products in the past and I had a lot of intellectual property, there were much bigger things to come.

For the next two years I drove back and forth from Oregon to California to spend days, weeks, even months with my mother. There were times when she was very functional, others when she lay near death in the hospital, and everything in between. For years I had searched for my purpose, only to discover that my greatest purpose was serving my mother at the deepest level a child can. I was able to put into practice over thirty years of spiritual studies. I completely trusted that if I showed up to my greatest calling, all would work out. I discovered what it really meant to let Source work through me.

Each day I would ask to be guided as I traveled that uncharted territory. It was not always easy. There were days I wanted to pull the covers over my head and make it all go away. But each day I woke to the reality that my mother was very sick and needed me.

I knew I needed to keep my business going, too. Fortunately I had the foresight to know it would not be business as usual. I had made great revenue up to that point through various avenues online including speaking engagements, writing books, creating products, hosting teleseminars, affiliate marketing, and aligned partnerships. I knew that my knowledge could and would make a difference for many entrepreneurs.

With a mortgage to pay, a slew of animals to feed, and a partner who depended on our business revenue to maintain our lifestyle, I had to figure out what was to come next. It was a blessing to already have in place a formula for creating revenue streams that would actually grow my business while I took care of my mom. If I hadn't previously laid that powerful foundation to position myself as an expert in product creation, the outcome would have been incredibly different.

With the willingness to make the necessary changes and do what I needed to do, I was able to generate multiple streams of revenue while fulfilling my role as one of my mother's primary caretakers. I became more committed than ever to teaching as many people as possible how to do the same by setting their businesses up to generate multiple streams of revenue while fulfilling a higher calling.

It's All about Focus

Our experiences are what move us into our life's work. The choice is whether to respond to whatever life throws at us in a proactive way and keep moving forward, or stay stuck and flounder about. Since you were attracted to this book, I know you want to move forward and fulfill your life's work. *Power Up for Profits* is the perfect vehicle to help you achieve your dreams and goals.

There are people fulfilling their life's work each and every day. Some are visible in the marketplace and others have a more low-key presence. Whether you want to become highly visible or create a small jewel of a business, there are strategies in this book for you. But it also takes a commitment to implementing them on a consistent basis to have the greatest impact.

The right focus, thoughts, beliefs, choices, and actions are essential to success. It's easy to find excuses and reasons why things can't be done, why they are not working, and why success eludes us. However, no matter how difficult your present circumstances, if you keep your focus on your vision you will have the energy to keep moving forward. Had I not kept my focus on what my mother needed instead of what I needed, I would definitely have given up.

Our life's work often resides within an obvious passion.

Take the case of top-ranked NFL tight end and 49ers star Vernon Davis, who also owns Gallery 85, an exclusive art gallery in Santana Row in San Jose, California. Gallery 85 offers a wide range of visual artists a venue for high-end exposure for their work while raising funds for the Vernon Davis Foundation for the Arts, which promotes arts education and art appreciation for at-risk youth and awards college art school scholarships for talented inner-city youth.

Some would say Vernon's life's work is to be a great tight end, while others would say it is running his nonprofit organization. Another perspective is that both are part of his life's work.

Then there's Tia Torres, an iconic figure who rescues pit bulls. What started as a part time interest in rescuing dogs has become Tia's life's work. Having worked as a gang counselor at one point in her career, her passion for rescuing animals turned into what is now known to millions as the TV show *Pit Bulls and Parolees.*

In the late 1990s, during a visit to a local animal shelter, Tia met a four-year-old pit bull who made a huge impression on her. She touched Tia's heart and was instrumental in Tia's pursuing her new calling. The journey to save pit bulls was a rough one with many obstacles along the way. But with her big "why" always in the forefront of her journey, Tia overcame incredible obstacles to become known as one of the most powerful dog rescuers of all time.

Because of Tia's work, thousands of pit bulls destined to be throw-away dogs now live in loving homes. Her work not only saved these amazing creatures, but she has transformed the misunderstanding people had about pit bulls into love.

It is now easier to get the word out about what Tia and others like her are doing to make a difference in the world. There have been amazing advances in communication technology since the time when she first began her rescue mission.

Whatever your calling, what is your bigger "why"? Certainly there are times when things get really tough for Tia Torres and her pit bull rescue program. What allows her to stay the course is that her commitment is bigger than her.

It's the same with Vernon Davis. At times there are likely challenges he must overcome to stay the course. Yet, he does. And through Internet and social media marketing he has been able to raise awareness about the needs of talented inner-city artists in a much bigger way.

We are often led to believe that there should be no struggles, no hardships, no obstacles in pursuing our dreams. Give me a break! There *will* be times when things are a challenge, and it is often the challenges that inspire us in our true calling.

Isn't This Supposed to Be Easy?

There has been so much hype about how easy things should be and that all we need do is visualize what we want and presto! it appears. Although I am a firm believer in the Law of Attraction, there have been major misunderstandings of what the law is about. It is about visualization, focus, and commitment. A great many people take initiative regarding visualization, but one needs focus and commitment to see the law through to its rewards.

Another aspect of the Law of Attraction is getting out of your own way and allowing events to unfold as they will. In many cases the outcome appears in ways we least expect it to. If, in fact, you have said you want to do your life's work in a big way, *Power Up for Profits* is definitely for you.

Rules regarding how we express who we are have changed dramatically over the last few decades. In the past we had to wait for permission to express ourselves – at least that's what we were led to believe. And believe this we did. Today, due to the outlets and avenues available (literally at our fingertips), we can express who we are, what our message is, and how we want to impact the lives of others in so many incredible ways. Our expression is limited only by our willingness to step up to the challenge.

You are limited only by your own limitations. The beauty of the tools we have available today is that anyone – yes anyone – can take massive action to get incredible results. You will experience the best results when you take a holistic approach to your business. For example, rather than classifying yourself as solely a consultant, why not think in terms of becoming an author, speaker, and mentor? By doing this you are more fully able to serve your market by packaging your information into a book that is easy to invest in and learn from. At the same time you help yourself as well. When you are a published author, you garner more respect because you are an expert who "wrote the book" on your topic. When you are viewed as an expert you are more in demand as a mentor and can command higher fees.

Today an expert can easily become an author and reach online bestseller status by way of strategic marketing and promotions. Experts can package their information into various types of products. It's possible to reach a global market as long as they have a computer and Internet access. Even senior citizens can begin their first business in their sixties, seventies, eighties – the sky's the limit.

Jane Falke is a nutritionist whose passion is teaching others about eating whole, natural foods. Jane spent over twenty years studying food and nutrition from a natural perspective. People often asked her when she was going to put her knowledge into a book.

Not only did Jane have her first book published at the age of seventy-one, she also committed to learning as much as she could about reaching her market through online marketing. She is the first to admit that getting her book published and gaining an online presence wasn't always a walk in the park, but it was worth it. Rather than being limited to sharing her message in her geographic region, she now has readers and clients around the globe.

If a woman in her seventies can get her first book to market and gain an online presence, don't you think you can, too? Of course you can!

By Design or Default?

For years I held back, thinking success was for others but not for me. It wasn't until I was willing to step out in a big way that things began to change. And change they did! I went from struggling day-in and day-out to having an abundance of money, business, and impact.

Not only had my fear held me back, but I now work with clients whose greatest fears show up in the most amazing ways. I have one client who had a major block in building an opt-in subscriber list. For weeks we explored strategies she could use to build her list. But all we seemed to do was talk about it until I confronted her about her fears. She had a huge breakthrough during a live mastermind session. As it turned out she feared rejection. It was more comfortable for her to not build her list and say how things weren't working than to build her list and risk being rejected by the very people who willingly got on her list. When she realized that not building her list was actually preventing her from impacting the very people she was most passionate about, she became willing to walk through her discomfort to get to the other side.

How often do we do this to ourselves? We say we want something but then do everything we can to sabotage our success. Sabotage comes in many shapes and forms: taking inappropriate action, not taking action, taking a little action but then dropping the ball, and on and on. What are you holding back on? What is your fear? What is your self-imposed limitation? You can live for "someday," or you can claim your spot right here, right now. The choice is yours.

Chapter 2

Marketing Foundation

Although I can't guarantee a particular amount of money you will generate with the information in *Power Up for Profits*, I can assure you that your results will be determined by how much effort you put into your success. The more sincere effort you put into the learning, development, and implementation of the information, the more you will get out of it and the quicker you will achieve your goals. What I can guarantee is this: The concepts will work for anyone who applies them. My goal and my responsibility are to help you succeed and make more money.

In this book you will learn how to identify customers and markets, stretch your marketing dollars, creatively position you and your business globally, and gain massive amounts of visibility within your market. You will learn to create public relations (PR) opportunities where none seem to exist; get your message to your market, often with little or no cost; develop a presence in your customer's mind even in your absence; maintain top-of-mind awareness; and develop a smooth-running PR machine for you and your company.

These are not theories from a textbook. These are proven strategies. I practice what I preach and consistently use these strategies to build my own publishing, consulting, speaking, and training businesses. I have used these strategies with countless clients to help them achieve amazing results. I have helped numerous companies use the step-by-step strategies to achieve awesome results.

Every Business Is a Sales and Marketing Business

No matter what your industry, who your market is, or what product you offer, your business is a sales and marketing business. Unfortunately a lot of entrepreneurs don't understand this, and even if they do, they resist it. "I feel like I'm prostituting myself," was the start of one conversation I had recently with a struggling energy worker. She truly believed that if she marketed her services she was somehow selling her soul to the devil. "No wonder you're struggling!" I responded. When I told her that marketing was simply ensuring that potential clients knew she existed, she relaxed.

The first place marketing should happen is in your mindset. If you don't have the right mindset, no matter what skills you learn you likely won't do very well. Focus on how to find the right market for your product while maintaining top-of-mind awareness. You want to occupy space in your customer's mind.

A Misconception about Marketing

Many think that sales and marketing has to be pushy. Nothing could be further from the truth. You simply need to make people aware of what you offer and create the opportunity for them to invest in what you offer based on their wants and needs. If you believe in what you do, you owe it to your market to let them know what you offer. To not do this is a disservice to your market.

Primary Reasons People Don't Succeed at Marketing:

➤ A misunderstanding of what marketing is and is not
➤ Fear of the unknown
➤ Not knowing what to do
➤ Not knowing who their target market is
➤ Trying to be all things to all people
➤ Using a shotgun approach
➤ Not budgeting for marketing
➤ Lack of time
➤ Poor planning
➤ Being too scattered
➤ Chasing after the next get-rich-quick scheme
➤ Trying to do it all themselves

If you want to succeed, there are some "must-knows" in regard to marketing:

➤ Who your market is
➤ How to market to them
➤ What the market perception of you and your business is
➤ Market trends impacting your industry
➤ How these components all fit together

Learning this information involves doing a proper analysis of your market, the product you need to create and offer, and the most efficient way to do this to generate high revenue and great profit margins. I'll show you how to accomplish all of those tasks in future chapters.

If the purpose of your business is to fulfill your life's work while contributing to the well-being of others, isn't it time to get serious about doing this? Haven't you been procrastinating long enough? Isn't now the time for you to increase your marketing knowledge and your ability to implement this knowledge? Believe it or not, marketing can be fun, fulfilling, uplifting, and impactful.

So let's begin with a clear definition.

Marketing is the process of raising awareness of your products and communicating their value to the end user.

Types of Marketing

In virtually any book about marketing, you typically learn about promotions and advertising. Thank goodness you chose to read this book, because my approach to marketing goes way beyond the typical to include:

➤ Internal marketing
➤ External marketing
➤ Online marketing
➤ Offline marketing
➤ Push/pull marketing
➤ Energy marketing, which includes your intention and using the Law of Attraction and visualization

All are necessary components of a wildly successful marketing program. But don't worry about how you will achieve every element; you'll know about all of these marketing strategies by the time you finish this book.

Internal Marketing

There are two types of internal marketing – the internal marketing of your business systems, and your internal guidance or intuitive process.

Internal marketing of your business systems is what you know about your company's infrastructure that your customers may not know. Without knowing the ins and outs of your company's infrastructure, it is nearly impossible to convey your strengths to the market. The more you know, the better you can position your message.

Your internal guidance has to do with the creative thoughts you have that you will either choose to act on, or not. Your success is determined by your ability to ascertain which thoughts are most beneficial to act on at any given time and which should be tabled for later exploration.

External Marketing

External marketing is what the world sees or perceives. It includes your:

➺ Advertising
➺ Website
➺ Blog
➺ Social media marketing
➺ Direct marketing
➺ Marketing material including business cards, letterhead, and logo
➺ Product development
➺ How you present yourself when out in public (your professionalism, attire, and grooming)

Does your external image match your internal reality?

External marketing is a direct reflection of how successful you will be. If you cut corners to save a few dollars, the image you project might not attract the market you are targeting. On the other hand, you can overinvest in external marketing if your target customer is a thrifty one.

How You Dress

What used to be considered the standard attire for success – a suit and tie for men and a dress or pantsuit for women – is no longer required. Today there are countless types of attire one can wear and still look professional. For example, if an artist were to wear a suit and tie in their business setting, they might look out of place. Your attire should match the image you want to project. In my case, I went from wearing business suits to jeans, blazers, nice blouses, and western boots. This fits my branding and my market. What image do you want to project and what will your market feel comfortable with? It's about being authentic. Don't try to be someone you're not. The market demands authenticity more each day.

This leads to the essential element of knowing who wants to do business with you and whom you want to do business with. You will learn how to identify your market in another chapter.

Push/Pull Marketing

Push/pull marketing is exactly what it sounds like. At times you are "pushing" information out to your market and at other times you are implementing strategies to "pull" (attract) consumers to you.

In the past, push marketing was the norm. Now, due to social media marketing, pull marketing is a huge aspect of successful marketing. Regardless of whether you are selling someone else's product (affiliate sales) or your own, the push/pull philosophy can reap better results with less work.

Market Consistently

To continually position your expert status and create a steady stream of revenue from your product, you have to have an extremely targeted approach. Not only will a systemized marketing approach help you make money directly from your online offerings, but it can enhance your offline offerings such as with live presentations, consulting, and coaching.

An important aspect of your marketing is consistency. Commit to doing something every single day. An on again, off again approach won't work. Your results are directly proportionate to your ongoing efforts.

The Purchasing Process

There is a process customers go through when buying your product. It is built on need and desire. The greater the investment on the part of your customer, the more you must build confidence, trust, and credibility in their mind. If you are selling $10 widgets, that's one thing. If, on the other hand, you are seeking to build long-term relationships with your customers and be viewed as the "go-to" expert, you need a systematic approach. While widgets are sometimes part of my clients' product offerings, they usually want to go beyond the widget and make a difference in the lives of their customers. They want to provide long-term solutions and create ongoing relationships with their customers. They want to build their business based on trust, value, and integrity.

No matter how great your product, most people will not buy a high-ticket product or a $1,000, $5,000, $10,000-plus mentoring course or consulting contract without first being introduced to you by way of a free or $20-$50 offering. This is what is referred to as "funnel marketing."

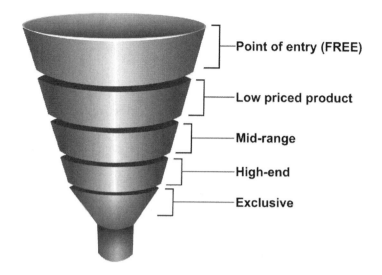

Point of entry (FREE)

Low priced product

Mid-range

High-end

Exclusive

Customers enter your funnel by way of something that is very low risk such as a free or very inexpensive item. Based on their experience with that first contact with you, they decide what their next course of action will be.

What you do every step of the way, including someone's initial introduction to you and your way of doing business, determines how likely it is that someone will become a loyal customer. Never discount the power of a free offering or a low-ticket item to be the catalyst for someone's becoming a premier client. A great majority of the clients who pay me tens of thousands of dollars a year started by way of something free or very low cost.

I positioned my expertise, gained their trust, delivered above and beyond expectations, and the rest, as they say, is history. But – and this is a big but – I had a way to get them into my sales funnel.

One of my favorite TV shows is *Shark Tank.* The premise of the show is a budding entrepreneur pitches an idea to four extremely successful entrepreneurs who make millions upon millions in their own businesses. There is a long, arduous process that contestants go through to be on *Shark Tank.*

In addition to possibly getting funding for their idea, contestants are seen by millions of viewers. Imagine the opportunity to gain market reach if you and your business were seen by millions of prospective customers and clients.

What blows me away is how unprepared most contestants are with their online presence. Out of all the people who appear on *Shark Tank*, only a handful have their websites optimized for new traffic. Most do not have a way for visitors to opt in for features on their websites, whether it be a coupon, a report, or a training video as it relates to their products and market need. Oy vey.

These people are seen by millions, yet they are not doing all they can to make their sites completely visitor-ready. Wake up, folks. If you've made it to *Shark Tank*, wouldn't it be a good idea to prepare your site for it?

You can bet lots of viewers are checking out contestants' websites on their iPads, iPhones, and laptops while watching the show. Imagine how many opportunities are missed if there isn't a way for someone to opt in. Ouch!

Just like the *Shark Tank* contestants, if you're not capturing contact information, visitors will likely never come back to your site and will soon forget about you – a harsh reality. Here's a simple rule: Have an opt-in opportunity with something of extremely high value for site visitors. When you have someone's email address, you can let them know about specials, discounts, and product bundles while continuing to create massive value for your subscribers.

Once someone opts in, continue to create high value as well as offer products they would benefit from. If you've been looking for a simple solution for how to increase revenues you generate from your site, I just gave it to you.

Far too often people say, "My business is not working." Yet when they are given the solution for what to do, they don't take advantage of it. For example, there was one *Shark Tank* participant I had a phone conversation with after he appeared on the show. He was frustrated that he didn't get the funding he had hoped for, and his site wasn't selling much at all. Within seconds I identified a few glaring problems with his site.

I told him I wanted to use his site as a case study for a group of my high-level clients. I wanted to show them a few simple changes that would make the site a money magnet. "Absolutely," he said without hesitation. I created a short screen-capture video in which I pointed out the most obvious steps he could take to improve conversions. The video was made available to my private clients as well as to the owner of the site.

The guy got really excited about the information, saying he was going to update his site as soon as possible. One change would have been very simple: offer a gift such as a report, short video, or MP3 that visitors would opt in for. Another was to offer a fabulous special for *Shark Tank* viewers and make it super easy and very low risk for people to make their first purchase. The site owner received the video about six months ago. Not one change has been made.

Mind you, if he would have said, "I'm not interested. I have no desire to change things. Beat it," I would be fine with that. But he got really excited by my offer, said he didn't know much about using the Internet to market his business, and welcomed my recommendations. So why hasn't he updated his site? Simple. He's not convinced it's worth the effort. Or worse yet, he is so caught up in the details of his business he is missing the big picture.

Considering that online purchases during the 2012 holiday season were up considerably from 2011, there is massive opportunity for online retailers. Retail web sales increased 12 percent and surpassed $92 billion according to Shop.org, the digital division of the National Retail Federation trade group. The increase covers shopping during November and December of 2012.

Forester Research says that e-retail spending will increase 62 percent by 2016 and U.S. consumers will spend $327 billion online in 2016. Most consumers are choosing the Internet to purchase what they want. For an entrepreneur not to have their site fully optimized (especially when millions of eyes will be seeing what they offer) is crazy.

If you're not doing everything you possibly can to ride this ever-increasing wave, you'll soon be left behind. Position your expertise at various entry points. To introduce customers to you and your product offerings, and get people to consider your free or $20 item, you will find the push/pull marketing process second to none. The higher the price of your product, the more the push/pull strategy pays off.

Push Marketing

Online push marketing is literally "pushing" information to your market. It begins by getting someone on your opt-in subscriber list as we just discussed. Push marketing includes interviews, articles, blog updates, videos, ezines, daily tips, special reports, postings on social networks and forums, and invitations to teleseminars and webinars. The idea is that once someone is on your list, you send valuable information to them on a consistent basis so they become familiar with you, your name is recognizable, and you build trust.

The more your market knows, likes, and trusts you, the easier the sales process is. Equally important is perceived value. The more value they perceive, the easier it is to make a sale – that is, if they are your target market (your ideal client). All the value in the world to a mismatched market will do you (and them) no good. On the other hand, the more value you create for the correct market, the more your subscriber list and revenues will grow.

One of my clients was in the middle of a huge identity shift and life change when we first began working together. In years past she had built a business that made over $400,000 per year. Over a period of three years her revenue decreased by over 75 percent. Frustrated, she needed to make drastic changes. Good thing she recognized this, because she was likely to run her business into total collapse if she hadn't.

Time was of the essence to get her new message out to market. Not only was time important, so was her own personal shift in perception. She had to be willing to let go of who she used to be and embrace who she was becoming. In the first few months of her transition we had many conversations about the fact that there would be a drop-off of some of her previous clientele who simply did not resonate with the new persona she was presenting to the world. Yet on the flip side, there were many of her clients who absolutely loved the change, and a new group of people flocked to her message.

As you change, there's a strong possibility your market and offerings will change. Be prepared for this. It can be very emotional to watch clients you thought appreciated you leave your tribe. Do not let this stop you from embracing your new direction. Fair warning: you will experience the temptation to stay in a neatly wrapped box. Your job is to let go of the past, embrace the future, and be willing to risk going into the unknown. It has been said, "With risk comes reward."

As these changes occur, so must the information you offer to your market. A goal in push marketing is to continually provide timely, quality information and high-perceived value in order to develop a loyal consumer base. Etch that last sentence in stone – it is so incredibly important.

Building an opt-in subscriber list is one very important way to provide value to your prospects and control when they receive it. Although a large, targeted opt-in subscriber list is desirable, some people have had great financial success with lists of just a few hundred people due to the quality of the list and the size of their offerings.

One colleague of mine tells the story of how she generated over $100,000 with a list of 561 subscribers. This is almost unheard of, and flies in the face of all those who say the size of the list is all that matters. In reality, the *quality* of the list is what's most important. Quality and size makes a winning combination.

Another colleague has a list of 2,500, and in 2012 generated over $400,000. You read right – four hundred thousand dollars.

There is a huge misunderstanding that a massive list is what you should strive for. A *responsive* list is what you truly need. The ideal scenario is a large, responsive list. The secret to success is to nurture your list and continually bring value to your subscribers based on what you offer and what they need, want, and are willing to pay for.

Active participation in the right social networks is yet another aspect of push marketing. You will learn a great deal in future chapters about social networks and social media marketing.

Pull Marketing

As the name implies, pull marketing is persuading consumers to visit your various online locations to get them to either buy something or subscribe to your opt-in list. It is about generating traffic to your website, blog, and landing pages.

Most people will not buy something on their first visit to your site, blog, or landing page unless it is incredibly low-priced and low-risk. When you minimize the risk to your visitors, they are more inclined to take an initial small step. The less risk, the more likely it is that you will engage your visitor. Minimal risk would be providing their name and email address for a free report, white paper, ezine, video, teleseminar, webinar, daily or weekly tips, an ebook, or a podcast. Another way to minimize risk is to offer a high-quality guarantee, which actually reverses risk.

Be careful not to overwhelm your subscribers with too much unnecessary email. Consumers have become so overwhelmed with the amount of follow-up email they receive when they opt in for a free offer that they often use a secondary email account just for registering for information. Many download something and immediately opt out of the very list they requested to be added to.

This means your offering must be of such high value that subscribers will want to continue to receive whatever follow-up information you offer. Don't offer just anything to get that email address, offer something that will impress your target market. As in the world of offline marketing, first impressions are lasting impressions.

Offering something of extremely high value will easily set you apart from the countless others trying to accomplish the same thing that you are – increasing your customer base and revenue stream. Adopting a long-term perspective on what you have to offer can create the kind of value consumers have grown to not only want, but demand.

The best part of pull marketing is that it both builds your subscriber list and raises awareness through your promotions. Many of the strategies you use to promote your expertise are the very same strategies used to build your opt-in subscriber list: article marketing, blogging, media releases, joint-venture campaigns, email signature (sig) files, and forum group participation.

Making push/pull marketing a part of your everyday efforts optimizes opportunities. The more consistent you are, the quicker your results will be.

Know Your Market

Regardless of how much or how little marketing knowledge you have, it is essential to always know who your market is and is not. It's also important to accept that your marketing strategy should change as your business changes. And of course you must know your limitations in terms of budget, time, and resources.

When I started my business in 1994, I dealt primarily with a corporate client base. Today I work primarily with solopreneurs and microbusinesses. Although the essence of how I market is strikingly similar to what it was in the nineties, the message is different.

Who do you want to do business with, and who wants to do business with you? What sets you apart from your competition? What is your unique selling proposition? These elements of your market should be continually reevaluated.

What motivates your market to take action? In most cases it boils down to four primary motivations: increasing revenues, increasing productivity, decreasing costs, and/or increasing the quality of their personal or professional life.

I offer my high-end clients a VIP Day (VIP=Very Important Person). The client and I spend a full day together developing a strategy for their business. I begin the process by having them identify their goals for the day. This can include things like developing a plan, identifying products they can take to market, clarifying their message, and determining what can be outsourced.

In a recent VIP Day, my client said she wanted to be able to have a good night's sleep. I knew that if we were able to identify some essential aspects of her business and what she could immediately do to generate revenue she would sleep better. A couple of days later she called to say, "I had the best night's sleep I've had in a long, long time." Although I didn't directly give her a better night's sleep, by virtue of what we were able to identify for her business, much of the pressure was lifted, resulting in better sleep.

The better you can pinpoint specifically what your clients want, need, and are willing to pay for, the easier the job of developing and delivering your product becomes.

Avoid Common Pitfalls

Without a clear understanding of your market and what you have to offer them, you may make some of the common mistakes inherent in running a business. Targeting the wrong market can make you come across as interested only in the sale rather than in your customer's needs. You might appear desperate by not being willing to let go of a potential or existing client when the fit is incompatible. And you might be unprepared when an opportunity to motivate your ideal customer presents itself.

Years ago I consulted with a high-end dental lab. Their clients were dentists who offered cosmetic dentistry to their patients. One of the most memorable stories I heard from the general manager was about when she worked for a dentist in Montana. A rancher in his sixties who wore bib overalls everywhere he went came in for a consultation to see about having a full set of veneers. The investment was going to be well over $50,000. Many people would have judged this man's ability to pay for this type of service based on his appearance. As it turned out, once the dentist was consulted and the price was established, the rancher left and returned a short while later with cash in hand to pay in full for the veneers.

The general manager said she learned long ago not to judge a potential patient by their appearance. However, they did do some preliminary work to establish whether the rancher was indeed a good fit for their services.

Avoid trying to sell something before establishing whether your product truly offers the best solution. Be careful not to prejudge a person's ability and motivation to buy. And don't compromise your core values by forcing a sale rather than attracting business through the Law of Attraction. When your values are in alignment with your market, your offerings, and your message, the process of growing your business becomes a flowing experience. That is not to say there is no effort involved; quite the opposite. But things begin to flow and feel effortless a great deal of the time.

Energy Marketing

Energy marketing is an energetic connection with your marketing and sales. It is one thing to learn the mechanics, skills, and steps of marketing; it is something completely different to go beyond the surface level and truly "connect" with your market. I am convinced that much of effective marketing occurs on an invisible and subconscious level.

You can take all the "right" action steps, but if you don't believe in what you are doing, don't feel deserving, have prosperity issues, or have a habit of sabotaging your success, you may need to focus on energy marketing. Pay attention to what you say to yourself and others about the economy, business, and your own situation. Notice the thoughts that come up throughout your day, the conversations you have with others, and whether you are supporting a success posture or one that does not serve you. Surround yourself with others who also want to succeed in business. Join mastermind groups, get mentors, and read books that will keep you focused on positive visions.

Keys to Successful Marketing
- → Focus on serving your market and solving their problems.
- → A profitable volume of sales is a better goal than just trying to get more sales. If you have not determined your ideal profit margins, you could actually be losing money with each sale.
- → Determine the needs of your customers through market research. Then decide on specific markets to target and determine what product will satisfy their needs.

Market Positioning
To achieve the outcomes you desire you must put your stake in the ground through market position, meaning stand up for what you believe. Don't be wishy-washy; stand tall and proud and be willing to do what needs to be done to let people know you exist.

When you first begin your business, you may not have the confidence you will gain over time regarding how you market you, your products and services, and your business. The sooner you get comfortable with marketing, the better. One of my goals in this book is to cut years off the time it takes you to gain a high level of confidence. There is a direct correlation between your level of confidence and the amount of money people will pay for your expertise. There is also a direct correlation between what people will pay you and how your expertise is packaged. Given two experts with equal qualifications including years in the industry, education, and knowledge, and one has taken time to package their knowledge into books and information products and the other has not, the first will command more money for their expertise.

When customers and prospective customers think of products like yours, you want to be the one who comes to mind and the one they will do business with. This top-of-mind awareness is known as *market position.*

Market position is achieved through branding, packaging, public relations, promotions, a unique selling proposition, and excellent customer care, to name just a few. In the online world, there are four primary ways to become top-of-mind:

➤ Build celebrity position
➤ Become active in social networks
➤ Use online media opportunities
➤ Develop aligned partnerships

Celebrity Position

By celebrity position I am not referring to Oprah-level celebrity. Celebrity in this context is becoming incredibly visible and well-known to your market.

Social Networks

Involvement in social networks is a must-do! You cannot escape it. But ensure that your involvement is effective and not a waste of time.

Online Media

Over the past few years, media opportunities have cropped up all over the Internet – everything from online magazines to blogs, Internet radio, video sites, and social media. Many of these opportunities cost nothing but time. It's amazing how much visibility a targeted approach will get you with online media.

Aligned Partnerships

One of the fastest ways to build celebrity is through the partnerships you develop. No one makes it on their own. Successful people build solid relationships with others who support their values.

Although we have become an instant gratification world, there are those who know that success is not an overnight happening. To truly succeed in any venture, especially building your business using the strategies in this book, it takes time, commitment, and focus. Lay a solid foundation and you are in a great position to reap fantastic benefits.

To succeed you must have a long-term view as well as short-term goals. Get into the game of using the Internet to build your business and market position with the knowledge that this does take effort, work, investment, and time. When you do, you are way ahead of the majority of people who attempt this for a little while only to give up when they realize it is real business at its best.

Chapter 3

Your Marketing Strategy

Understanding your unique selling proposition, analyzing the market, and identifying your target market – or ideal customer – are the steps to take *before* launching a marketing program. They will save you time, money, and frustration over the long run. Many people think they are saving time by immediately trying to gain market position, but doing this can derail your efforts. Let's take a look at who your market is, what your expertise is, and what your market's challenges are.

Step 1. Identify Your Market

You've probably heard this before: **When everyone is your market, no one is your market.** Often the people you want to sell to are people like you, so you imagine you know them well. But this is not always the case.

Target Market Analysis

Target market analysis tells you who needs and wants your product *and who can afford to buy it.* Plenty of people may want and need your product, but that doesn't mean they can afford to buy it. Matching your products to specific groups of people, and knowing the difference between each of these markets, is critical to penetrating existing markets and developing new markets. You must be able to match the product you offer to specific groups of people who are willing and able to buy the product. You must also know the differences of these target markets.

Don't limit yourself to one market; you may have several. Recently during an intensive VIP Day, my client discovered that she had three very unique markets – men and women who dream of starting a business, established small business owners, and franchise owners. Each market was unique, and she needed a different marketing strategy for each. You may have one product line that is more generic and less costly than another, so different people will buy that product than those who buy your more exclusive product – thus you have two different target markets.

Don't forget to assess the actual size of your market. Your market must include enough customers able to afford your product and willing to buy it in order for your business to thrive.

Niche Markets

A niche market is a narrowly defined group of potential customers that usually evolves based on demand for a specific product. Niche markets can arise from changes in society, technology, or fashion.

Product development for a niche market is the process of finding and serving pockets of customers in a profitable way by designing products custom-made for that market.

Niche markets can be more profitable than broad, generic markets even though they are so much smaller, and especially if you are viewed as an expert and go deep into the niche market with your offerings. Here are some examples:

Broad Market	Niche Market
Health products	Expert health services for those 100 or more pounds overweight
Dog training	Guard dog training
Caterer	Expert in catering weddings for 500 or more guests

The examples above hopefully spark ideas for how you can narrow the way you define your expertise and offerings.

Hot Tip: In the world of online niche marketing, a blog or website can be developed and promoted quickly to target and serve small markets of a loyal customer base.

Demographics Analysis

The demographics of your market are their geographic location, age, gender, family status, income, buying behavior, buying preferences, etc. Analyzing the demographics of your market helps you understand their behavior. Here are some essential questions for gathering demographics:

➡ What is their age group?

➡ What is their gender?

➡ What is their family structure (number of children, extended family, etc.)?

➡ What is their lifestyle like – active, sedentary, family-oriented, spiritual?

➡ Where do they live?

➡ What do they do for a living?

➡ What keeps them awake at night?

➡ How do they like to spend their spare time?

➡ What motivates them?

➡ What do they invest in specific to your offerings?

➡ What are they likely to spend money on?

➡ What is their annual income?

➡ What methods do they prefer for online payment?

➡ What types of websites, forums, and social networks do they visit?

➡ How do they want their product delivered?

➡ How many people make up this market?

Gathering Market and Customer Information

Obtaining customer demographics does not have to be difficult or costly. You can determine what your market wants by studying your own existing market or by studying a competitor's market and product. Gather information from places your market congregates:

» Social networks
» Online and offline media reports and stories
» Blogs concerned with market trends
» Conduct surveys of your market

Market Segmentation

As you develop your marketing strategy, keep in mind that you should market in different ways to different *segments* of your market. You cannot be all things to all people. Instead of marketing a product in one way to everyone, you may need to market differently to markets with different demographics. Regardless of your product, divide your total market into segments according to what is important to each demographic group.

A couple of years ago I developed an information program that taught how to develop information products. When I launched my product-creation course, I started by offering a free video series on how to develop profitable products. I did the same thing when I developed a list-building program; I offered a free video series on list-building. Each free offer attracted thousands of new subscribers. Some people got on both lists, while a great many did not.

With two very different product offerings, it was essential to segment the subscriber list. Market segmentation enables you to target different categories of customers who perceive the value of certain products differently from one another. I divided the list into list-building contacts and product-creation contacts according to what people opted in for, and maximized my marketing efforts by fully customizing follow-up messages for each segment of my main list. When you don't segment your market, you experience more opt-outs.

More Demographic Terms

Psychographics

Characteristics of customers based on ideology, values, beliefs, and attitudes.

Predisposition

The likelihood that someone will make a particular purchase based on their culture, background, or upbringing.

Influences

Circumstances that affect someone's decision to buy such as education, religion, political affiliation, or peer pressure.

Lifestyle

How your market conducts their daily lives – liberal or conservative? Young or old? Active or sedentary? Gay or straight? Religious, spiritual, or neither?

Product Attributes

Product attributes are the features and benefits that make a product appealing to the customer. One of the most important requirements is that it fulfills a need or desire.

Customers buy a product based on whether it will improve the quality of their personal or professional life, increase their income, increase their productivity, and/or decrease their costs. To attract customers you must show them your product has a competitive advantage, is better in some way than your competitors' products, and/or provides a solution they seek. Otherwise, why would they do business with you?

It may be necessary to hire a market assessment expert to gather this information, but many solopreneurs can do it themselves by surveying their market, examining their competition's products, reading the latest news about their industry, and studying industry trends at social networks.

Step 2. **Identify Your Expertise and What Makes You Stand Out**

The best way to influence people's buying choices is to offer something they can only get if they work with you or buy your product or those you recommend. What is your expertise? What sets you apart from others? And why should prospects choose you over your competition? This is a portion of what will define your *unique selling proposition* (USP).

Every so often some "expert" claims we don't need a USP. Or they come up with some fancy-dancy name for it. But your USP is what makes you unique, which I feel is key to success. By identifying your USP you are able to more fully position your message. Granted, it's okay to blend in, but it's far better to stand out by taking a stand with your USP.

If you don't identify what makes you unique, your market won't be able to either. Without a unique flavor to what you do you are simply a commodity. The more of a commodity you are viewed as, the less value you can bring to your market. To gain clarity on your unique positioning statement, answer the following questions:

➻ What makes you unique?
➻ What do you do that others don't?
➻ What experience do you have that others don't?
➻ What results have you achieved that others have not?
➻ What specialized training or certification do you have that sets you apart from your competition?
➻ What beliefs and values do you stand by that set you apart from others?
➻ What irks you about your market?
➻ What are you committed to providing a solution for?
➻ What is your big *why* that drives you?

As you identify what sets you apart, be thinking in terms of a short identifying statement. Your USP is a strong, concise, simple statement about your business or brand that tells prospective customers why you are the best choice for them. Your USP very clearly answers the question, "Why should people do business with me and/or my company?" Here is mine:

> Kathleen Gage is the "no-nonsense, common sense" speaker, author and product creation specialist, and owner of the highly successful company Power Up For Profits. Kathleen helps entrepreneurs make money online. Her clients are driven by making a difference through their own unique voices.
>
> Considered to be one of the nation's most passionate speakers, Kathleen is known for cutting through the fluff and helping people leave their sob stories behind so they can stop focusing on the past and start looking toward the future. She speaks and teaches about what she believes are the core elements of a successful life: accountability, integrity, honesty, and living with passion and hope.
>
> Kathleen's mission is to help people understand that their business is merely a means to get their message out to the world. She teaches that it's not just about what you do, but the reasons behind why you do it.

Having a clear USP makes it easier to focus on both your product and the needs of your clients. If you have business partners, employees, subcontractors, or virtual assistants, a clearly defined USP makes it easier to get your team on board with your vision. They can understand your vision, be able to focus their energy on reaching the goals you have established for your business, and respond to inquiries appropriately.

Whenever a customer needs the type of product you sell, your USP should bring your company immediately to mind.

Finding Your USP

The whole idea of a unique selling proposition is to focus on what specific product your company provides. Find a niche or specialty that you can – or do – fill. It's difficult to operate a business without a clearly defined message. Many companies flounder because they do not have a clear message to convey; their products are mired in a state of ambiguity.

Begin by writing down every reason you can think of as to why people would want to do business with you. If your business involves others, include them in this exercise. You can have a high-energy brainstorming session that includes input from a cross section of people in your organization. You never know where some of the best ideas will come from within your group.

If you are a solopreneur, and belong to a mastermind group, you can brainstorm with those in your group. Mastermind groups are great for more than ideas; often you can also find business partners, vendors, customers, and joint-venture and affiliate partners.

Keep your customers in mind. Are they upscale, and price is not an issue for them? Or are they bargain hunters, and the best value for their money is most important to them? If money is not an issue for your market, and you are constantly offering sales and discounts, this could actually be counterproductive. If your market is price conscious, ignoring pricing issues is counterproductive.

Whatever answers you come up with regarding what makes you unique, follow up with the next question. For example, if you decide great service is what makes you unique, the next question is "What makes our service so great compared to our competitors?"

Some ways to differentiate your product from others are:

➡ How long you've been in the industry
➡ Life experience
➡ Price
➡ Convenience
➡ Whether your product is one-of-a-kind
➡ Expertise

➤ Track record
➤ Education
➤ Lack of education
➤ Certifications

Whatever USP you adopt, it's imperative that it resonates with who you really are.

Competitive Strengths and Weaknesses

Another very important aspect of identifying your expertise is determining your own strengths and weaknesses and those of your competitors. This allows you to know your true position in the market.

Some people (especially those who identify as highly spiritual) have a difficult time with the words *competitor* and *competition*. In this context a *competitor* is simply someone (or some company) who targets the same market you do.

It is crucial to be completely and totally honest about your strengths and weaknesses. Don't overlook this step, especially when it comes to weaknesses, because you will want to find ways to compensate for them in order to fully serve your clients. For example, if your weakness is not having the time or skill to write your own advertising copy, you can hire someone to handle this. If you are not a techno whiz, you should get help with that. Acknowledging where you lack skill, knowledge, or experience is more productive than trying to be someone who wears all the hats.

If you are just starting your business, you may not have the budget to outsource the tasks you are weak at, but as you grow your business it will become necessary in order to continue growing and remain on the leading edge. A year after I began my business, my partner, Karen, left her job to join my business. It was a big risk for us, but I knew that if we were going to grow the business, I couldn't continue doing everything myself. Karen's primary roll was layout and design work. When we saw that the Internet was going to be a part of what we were doing, she enrolled in a tech school to learn website design, among other skills. This was a huge investment for us at the time, but allowed us to do our own web work for the next fifteen years – definitely a good investment. Today we have a team of five people we outsource work to, including much of our web design work.

A weakness I had for many years was keeping too much in-house. Today I have turned that weakness into a strength by outsourcing a great deal of the day-to-day tasks that Karen and I both used to do. Knowing how to turn your weaknesses into strengths gives you a competitive advantage when negotiating high-end contracts.

Know Your Competitors' Strengths and Weaknesses

It is very helpful to know almost as much about your competitors as you do about your own company and customers. Unfortunately, many entrepreneurs don't take the time to find out about their competitors until it is too late. Knowing your competitors' strengths and weaknesses puts you in a better position to compete by marketing more effectively, and helps you find potential partnerships.

Often the very people who are your greatest competitors can make incredible partners. Such was the case with me and Lori Giovannoni. Though I considered her to be one of my biggest threats when it came to securing speaking contracts within specific markets, there came a day when we both realized we could bring more to some of our clients by collaborating on projects.

Lori and I gained a reputation for bringing incredible value and energy to events where we shared the platform. With the success we experienced by joining forces, we also secured a few consulting contracts together in the Salt Lake market. From there we partnered on some writing projects including the book *101 Ways to Get Your Foot in the Door: Success Strategies Guaranteed to*

Put You Miles Ahead of the Competition.

What started as a way to more fully serve our clients turned into a life-changing experience when Lori's world turned upside down. It was this situation that solidified the belief that your greatest competitors can turn out to be your most amazing collaborators. It allowed us to collaborate on the book *The Law of Achievement: Discover Your Purpose, Possibility and Potential.*

The following is from the foreword of *The Law of Achievement:*

> The idea for this book began many years ago as a result of numerous conversations. Having both achieved multiple levels of success, we wanted to share with others what achievement meant to us. Although we knew someday we would write the book we were continually sidetracked with never-ending professional endeavors.
>
> We went from *thinking* about writing the book to *being guided* to write the book through one event that changed the course of many lives. It is through this event our belief that the *only point of power is in the now* was reinforced like never before.
>
> At 6:19 pm on September 2, 2005, our world stopped. Troy Roper Jr., Lori's husband and Kathleen's dear friend, was in a severe motorcycle accident. The pursuit of business, joint ventures and material concerns came to a screaming halt.
>
> For 102 days our lives revolved around the shock trauma unit, surgery, intensive care, doctors, nurses and an endless stream of visitors and well-wishers. Lori slept in Troy's room every night and Kathleen relieved Lori every day.
>
> There was no word or concern about business issues. Priorities were rearranged and the world had shifted on its axis. When the crisis subsided it was evident we all had changed. Our beliefs and values had been tempered and some of them changed completely. Our greatest lesson and realization is that far too often we had lived in *"someday."*

Troy's accident reminded us to live in *today*, cherishing each moment. After over eight months of recovery, Troy continues to inspire us.

People tend to put off until "someday" what they really would like to do today. The delays come for many reasons. Time, money, laziness, no sense of urgency or just plain not getting around to it.

Starting as a *someday* project that we dabbled with for years, Troy's accident transformed this book into a *today* project. When we sat down to write *The Law of Achievement*, we knew it was destined to be a book that impacted many and made a difference not only to its readers but to people outside of the traditional business market.

This definitely shows that even our greatest competitors can become our most valued partners.

Step 3. **Know What Keeps Your Customers Awake at Night**

Knowing what worries your customers is essential in providing them with solutions. What are their most challenging problems? What drives them? What are their dreams and goals? And most important, what keeps them awake at night?

Before I work with my high-end clients, I have them complete an in-depth questionnaire that allows me to more fully understand their goals, dreams, current position, and challenges. This information puts me in a much better position to help them gain the success they desire. It also helps me disqualify those individuals who are not a good fit for my high-end programs.

Why in the world would you want to disqualify someone? It's simple; the better match someone is for what you have to offer, the better you can actually serve them.

Pay attention as well to what your customers have very *little* interest in. A few years ago I was in search of a very specific type of car. I wanted a Cadillac CTS. At that time I was not planning on buying a new one; I wanted one only a few years old and in great shape. Once the search began, I quickly realized that many salespeople do not listen to what a customer wants. Regardless of how clear I made it that I wanted a CTS, each salesperson attempted to sell me something else.

I recall one gentleman who said he was very certain he could find the car I was looking for. I was ecstatic when he called me to say, "I found a perfect car for you." I asked what color the CTS was and he said, "Oh, it's not a CTS, but I know you will love it." I couldn't believe what I was hearing. He completely ignored my wishes and tried to convince me I wanted something else. Needless to say I didn't buy my CTS from this man.

After owning my first CTS for six years, I was ready to get a newer model and decided this time it would be brand new. There was a marked difference in my experience. The sales professional I decided on focused on what I was most interested in about the car rather than showing me features that were not at the top of my list. When I drove away in my new car, I felt like a million bucks. I had been validated in *my* desires and not those of the salesperson.

Pay attention to your customers' needs and desires to assure your business success.

Chapter 4

Do They Know
Who You Are?

The Benefits of Gaining Visibility

The easiest way to build your business is to build your visibility. It makes little difference what industry you are in – visibility reigns.

Those who are making a living by way of the Internet are always on the lookout for how to increase their visibility. The more visibility you have that builds market recognition, the more your credibility as an expert in your field increases.

Gaining visibility is actually quite simple, but not always easy. If you don't know who your market is, you can spin your wheels trying to gain visibility in front of the right potential buyers. Before investing time and money in gaining visibility, first identify your tribe. To not do so is counterproductive.

Here's a simple fact: Visibility creates ample opportunities. Because of the Internet there are now countless ways to position your expertise and product. The more visible you are, the more opportunities seem to come out of the woodwork. You can never know the long-term impacts of creating an effective presence on the Internet.

Because of all the marketing I have done and the hundreds of interviews, articles, and teleseminars I have participated in, it is not uncommon for me to receive requests to participate in anthology books, telesummits, and joint-venture book launches. And I am frequently invited to do interviews and presentations at industry conferences. I used to say yes to just about everything, never knowing where the yes would lead.

As my business has grown, I have much more clarity regarding what I will and will not say yes to. Yet for anyone who is just starting out and wants to get a lot of experience, I usually recommend saying yes to more than you say no to.

I have a list of criteria I now use before I say yes: the person requesting my participation is very well positioned, the opportunity will generate business, I will be able to share the platform with other top experts, or all of the above.

A couple of years ago I got a call from a gentleman named Steve Olsher. Although I had never heard of Steve, he shared his plan for his book *Internet Prophets: The World's Leading Experts Reveal How to Profit Online.* His vision sounded exciting. Agreeing to be interviewed for a chapter, I asked Steve how he came to find out about me and why he selected me to be in his book. "You have a great reputation online. I asked several people if they knew any women online marketers, and your name came up from almost every person."

What this told me was that the years of effort I put into gaining visibility had paid off. Not giving the book much thought after the interview, Steve contacted me a few months later to tell me he was hosting an event by the same name, Internet Prophets, in Chicago. He wanted me to be one of the featured speakers along with the likes of Larry Winget, Armand Morin, Mike Filsaime, Mike Koenigs, Janet Bray Attwood, Marc Ostrofsky, John Kremer, Dan Hollings, and dozens of other experts.

Agreeing to join in on the festivities, I looked forward to personally meeting many of the experts I had admired for years, in particular Janet Bray Attwood, *New York Times* bestselling co-author of *The Passion Test: The Effortless Path to Discovering Your Life Purpose.* The event was beyond compare. By far it was one of the best events I had attended or spoken at. I made sure to be in the main ballroom for Janet Bray Attwood's presentation.

The event was the catalyst for Janet and me to meet face to face. Not only did we meet, we both felt like we had known each other for years. An immediate friendship developed, as did discussions on collaborating on future projects.

The point of sharing this with you is to emphasize the importance of continually getting your name out to your market. Had I not done all I had over the years, I never would have gotten the call from Steve. Had I not accepted Steve's invitation, I would not have been a contributing author for *Internet Prophets,* nor would I have met Janet. And who knows where our friendship and professional relationship will take us?

If this doesn't convince you that you need to take daily action in gaining visibility, I don't know what will.

You now possess the book that will show you how to gain massive visibility. Throughout the coming pages you will learn dozens upon dozens of ways to position your expertise, your message, and your business.

Know Your Big Why

There will be times when you'll wonder whether what you are doing is actually working. Sometimes you'll get immediate results, but that's often not the case. It's important to be consistent in getting your message and your name out to your market. Often what you did months or even years ago pays off.

Remember push/pull marketing? It's a process, not a one-time effort. It should become part of who you are. To stay motivated it is imperative to know "your big why." During the time I was my mother's caretaker, having the time to be with her was my big why. Today my big why is helping as many boomer entrepreneurs as I can set up their businesses in a way that gives them the freedom to live the lifestyle they either need or choose.

Another why in my business is that the more financial abundance I have, the more I can bless others. Whether it be buying grocery gift cards for family members in need, happily paying our handyman and being able to hire him for whatever our next project is, gladly paying our gardener, taking great care of our slew of rescue animals, or donating to nonprofit organizations I believe in, a successful business allows me to do this.

What is it that drives you in business? What is the message you want to share? Keep your big why in the forefront of all you do. Write it out and keep it visible. Regardless of what your message is, be proactive in getting the word out, and build trust with your market.

As you get your message out, stay focused on driving traffic to your blog, website, and landing pages in order to build your opt-in subscriber list. Often what you do to market is the very same thing you do to build your subscriber list. And be thinking about how to apply your list-building strategy to marketing other aspects of your business.

The Good, the Bad, and the Ugly

Although gaining visibility is a plus, there is a price to pay as you are known by more people. I would be doing you a disservice if I didn't share the downside of visibility. Granted, for most of us there is more of an upside, but you need to weigh the pros and cons as you move forward.

The best way to deal with the downside of visibility is to keep your focus on your big why. Wayne Dyer put it best when he said, "If there are 500 people in my audience, there are 500 opinions of who I am and the job I did." I've paraphrased a bit, but you get the idea. No matter what you do, you're not going to please everyone. This is especially true in the world of online marketing. If your goal is to make everyone happy you ought to quit right now. I'm serious. No matter what you do you are NOT going to please everyone.

When it comes to digital products and online marketing, decide right now that you are willing to take some criticism, because it's going to happen. Don't delude yourself into thinking you will never set yourself up for criticism. The fact is, the more visible you are, the more risks you take, the more you put yourself out there, the more of a moving target you are for anyone sitting behind a computer screen to shoot at any type of message that person chooses.

It's likely someone right now is saying, "Wow, you're being so negative." Then there are those who are smiling because they may have recently had something like this happen to them. I'm not writing this to be negative, but to provide a reality check to those people who think they will never receive criticism. When they do, they wonder what they could have done differently to not receive a nasty email, Facebook wall posting, or tweet.

It's not so much finding a way not to receive criticism. It's more about handling the criticism in a productive way. To assure you are on track with what you are doing as you gain visibility, here are a few simple guidelines:

- Know who your market is and is not. The clearer you are on this, the better. This way if someone who is not in your market lets off some steam, and you get the butt end of things, it really doesn't matter because they would never buy from you anyway.

- Give everything your very best. At the end of the day, when you know in your heart of hearts you've done the best you can, criticism is not going to have that much of an impact on you.

- Continue to study, learn, grow, and risk. Never, ever let a few bozos stop you from doing what you are passionate about.

- Surround yourself with others who will raise you up and at the same time push you to be even more than you currently are.

- Know what drives you. What is your big why? When you are clear on your why, it helps you to deal with adversity and frustration.

- Realize there are people who NEED what you have. To play small because of someone else's opinion, values, and beliefs is not only doing yourself a disservice, it's doing your tribe a huge disservice.

- Play big. Today we have opportunities to impact our markets like never before. The playing field has been leveled. What you do is determined more by your state of mind than by anything else.

We live in very exciting times. As previously mentioned, we have so much opportunity to impact our market like never before. The choice is yours how far you will go with this. Decide right here, right now, no matter what, that you will stay true to your course.

The Upside of Visibility

If you're still with me and accept that things won't always be a bed of roses, now you are ready for the fun side visibility.

Years ago I attended a conference with my sister. To avoid crowds we decided to register the night before the event began. There were a few other people who had the same idea. To say I was surprised when the first person I talked with, a woman from the Midwest, recognized me by my voice, is an understatement. This was the first of many people attending the conference who were either on my list, in one or more of my social networks, had read my articles, or had purchased products. Over the course of the three-day event I had a similar experience with others attending the conference. The best part of all of this were the invitations I received to be interviewed on radio shows and in written pieces as well as a couple of joint-venture opportunities that came out of these chance meetings. Had I not had the visibility I gained from my online presence, the outcome would have been different.

The more visibility you have, the more the doors open up. It's not uncommon when someone is planning a virtual event to base who they invite as an expert on how well-known the person is. And doesn't this make sense? A well-known expert draws in more viewers and listeners than an unknown.

Years ago I was the marketing advisor for a dentist in Pennsylvania. Dr. Capista had had a dream for a long time to share his business philosophy in a book. When *What Can a Dentist Teach You About Business, Life and Success* was published, we were very proactive in promoting the book through both online and offline media resources. Within a very short period of time interview requests became a very common occurrence. Out of these opportunities Dr. Capista secured speaking engagements, other interviews, and, best of all, new patients. It became obvious that these opportunities were a direct result of the efforts put into gaining visibility for his book.

Another client was pleasantly surprised when she received a call from one of the most influential men in the world of affiliate marketing to speak at his conference. I had worked with Cathy Demers on her market position with the goal of creating opportunities for her to speak at conferences. Obviously her efforts were paying off.

When Cathy arrived at the conference she was greeted by a small group of people who were very familiar with her work due to all she had been doing online. Over the course of the three-day event this became a common occurrence.

It turns out that Cathy's efforts with her Business Success Cafe® were incredibly popular and had positioned her very nicely for her appearance at the conference. Not only was her presentation at the conference a huge success, but several other opportunities opened up as a result including an invitation from the same gentleman to return the following year to present again.

After the first conference, multiple opportunities opened up for Cathy including more business online. She'll be the first to say it was a direct result of her visibility.

I can't overemphasize how essential visibility is. Throughout Power Up for Profits are various ways to achieve this. If you commit to implementing the ideas in this book into your standard business practices, you will be amazed at what is possible. In a matter of months you could feasibly go from total obscurity to an in-demand joint-venture partner, radio show host, conference speaker, and potential book contributor.

The possibilities are endless and ample. The key is taking action.

Chapter 5

Do You Know
What They Want?

It's likely your business is about providing solutions for your tribe. But before you can create the solution, you need to know what your market needs, wants, and is willing to pay for.

I'm always amazed at how often someone will create a solution before they understand the problem. Not only is this a waste of time, you could cost yourself countless dollars and untold frustration when people don't respond to your offers.

The solution? Find out what your market wants by asking. It's literally that simple. One of the best ways to do this is with surveys.

Conducting a Survey

A well-constructed survey reveals a great deal. You can conduct a "name required" survey or one that is completely anonymous. Respondents tend to be more frank and honest on anonymous surveys. It's as if they feel safer and tend to not hold back when they are not identified.

Surveys tell you what your market wants and how much they are willing to pay for it before you invest a lot of time and money developing products. They also provide fodder for articles, media releases, and blog postings based on what your market wants.

Unfortunately many professionals spend incredible amounts of time developing offerings based on what they *think* the market wants rather than what it *does* want. Survey, survey, survey – this is the magic word.

Keys to Successful Surveys
➼ Identify your objective
➼ Determine what information you need
➼ Develop the questions
➼ Conduct the survey
➼ Analyze the responses
➼ Develop products based on results
➼ Repeat

Identify your Objective

- Find out what is going on with your market
- Provide points of conversation with your market
- Determine what your market wants
- Discover your level of service based on your customer's perspective
- Learn more about demographic information – who your market is specifically
- Learn what you must prioritize based on market input

Determine What Information You Need

Determine what information is absolutely essential for you to know and what would be nice to know but is not essential.

Develop the Questions

Asking the right questions is one of the most important steps. Develop your questions based on your objective and what information you need to have. Don't avoid questions that you may be resistant to asking, such as "What area of our program is least helpful?" or "What can we do to improve our services?" Many people avoid asking such questions because they don't want negative feedback. But negative feedback is priceless; it allows you to improve on what you are doing.

Conduct the Survey

Before surveying on a large scale, you may want to test your survey with a small group of people. This helps you determine how effective and clear your questions are before investing in the larger effort. Be sure that those in your test market are representative of your real market. Surveying friends, family, neighbors, or anyone who is not in your market will not give you a true picture of what the problems are, what people are happy with, what their needs are, and where you need to focus your attention.

Analyze the Responses

Identify general themes, challenges, and interests based on responses. Use a program that allows you to run reports on your survey answers. For most solopreneurs and microbusiness owners, a service such as SurveyMonkey (www.surveymonkey.com) works just fine.

Develop Your Product Based on Results

Develop your product based on what your research determines. You should be able to determine pricing structures, delivery methods, frequency of offerings, and other pertinent information.

For the purpose of building a subscriber list, the survey results will provide insights as to what free offerings you need to create. Hitting the target with the right offers assures a greater number of opt-ins.

Survey results also enable you to develop marketing and sales messages using your customers' language. Pay close attention to the words people use in their responses.

Repeat as Needed

Products and services have lifecycles. As sales from your current offerings decline or you notice requests for items you don't currently offer, just repeat the above steps to gather more current information.

Knowing what is "hot" at any given time is simply a matter of researching your market. Find out what motivates them. For some it will be a high sense of values. For others it will be money, or status, or love. There are universal drives that are common to humans, and we all favor one or two of them over others. If you're not familiar with these, do a self-assessment to discover what your own preferences are. That will make it easier for you to identify and understand what motivates others.

Types of Questions to Ask:
» On a scale of 1 to 10, how important is_____ ?
» What is the most important part of training? (multiple choice)
» What is your single greatest challenge with_____ ?
» If you could solve one problem, what would it be?
» Give us your opinion on_____

Use the Likert scale:
   1 = Strongly disagree
   2 = Disagree
   3 = Neither agree nor disagree
   4 = Agree
   5 = Strongly agree

Demographic Information
Ask for demographic information such as age, gender, education, and geographic location.

Obtaining Responses
Although you can send out your survey in the body of an email, a service like SurveyMonkey™ can provide a more professional-looking and efficient survey. There are countless services available ranging from free to fee. I use the $20 per month SurveyMonkey service and have been pleased with the service. It is very easy to use and it's easy to analyze the results.

   Two of the most popular ways to post a survey are using a direct *uniform resource locator* (URL) and using *hypertext markup language* (HTML) that you add to your blog or website. A URL is a reference (address) to a resource on the Internet such as a website. HTML is the standard markup language for creating web pages and other information that can be displayed in a web browser. If you post your survey on your website or blog, make it visible enough and compelling enough for people to want to take it.

With some survey service providers you can get the HTML code to add to a specific location to "pretty up" your survey presentation.

The Survey Process in Action

The process for developing one of my most profitable membership programs about building a sustainable online business began with a simple survey. By conducting a survey *before* developing the program, I was able to design it to address the most important areas of interest. Based on initial responses I received about the program, I hosted a free preview call about building a sustainable online business. There was minimal risk in doing this, and a high probability of an excellent return on investment (ROI). Within forty-eight hours of announcing the preview call, "How to Build a Sustainable Six-Figure-a-Year Online Business," over 350 people registered for the call. I surveyed the 350 who had registered, and about 180 people responded – over 50 percent. (By the date of the call there were even more people registered.)

The responses not only provided a great indication of what I should teach on the preview call, they also gave me key information about what to offer in the membership program. Here's the information I gathered from the survey:

- ➨ 82.4 percent of those who responded made less than $100 per month online.
- ➨ 53.7 percent had been making money online for less than three months.
- ➨ The top three challenges for respondents were knowledge, budget to get the knowledge, and knowing who to trust.

This information proved to be very valuable; it was essential in the development of the membership program.

Distributing a Survey

Below are some of the best places to post your survey. Of course there are many more, but this will give you a great foundation for information gathering.

➤➤ Send to your current subscribers (if you currently don't have subscribers, when you apply the information in *Power Up for Profits* about list-building, you will have subscribers)

➤➤ Forums you belong to

➤➤ Google+ circles

➤➤ LinkedIn connections

➤➤ Your Facebook wall

➤➤ Twitter posts

➤➤ Yahoo groups

➤➤ Blog postings

➤➤ Articles with a resource box containing a survey link

➤➤ Signature (sig) file with survey link

➤➤ Create a short YouTube video with the survey link embedded in the video description

Create the Ethical Bribe

Once you have done your research, you'll be ready to create an ethical bribe, which is actually a free offer. Avoid falling into the trap of thinking you don't have time to offer something for free. Free ethical bribes are the cornerstone of building your online business.

There is never a shortage of emerging entrepreneurs who are afraid to give information away. "If I give my information away, nobody will want to buy what I offer" is the hard-held belief. This is absolutely not true. I have developed dozens of giveaways over the years – everything from e-reports to ebooks, teleseminars, ezines, four- and five-day email courses, video courses, and more. Doing so allowed me to build a subscriber list from the ground up (meaning I started with nothing and built a highly profitable list of subscribers).

The most successful among us started with nothing and built from there. And so can you! It should not require a lot of time on your part to fulfill a request for a giveaway. With the exception of a teleseminar, where you have dozens, hundreds, and even thousands of people on the call at one time, avoid offering a free session of your basic money-making service, such as free coaching time; you can cripple your business by having to be on the phone 24/7 fulfilling requests for free consulting.

With teleseminars and webinars you are delivering to everyone all at once, so this is a very effective use of your time.

Here are just a handful of ideas to get something free (your ethical bribe) to market quickly.

➤ Record an over-the-phone interview with an expert and give the recording away. (Be sure to get the expert's permission before giving away their information.)

➤ Write a tips list on a topic your market is interested in. (If you don't know what they're interested in, ask.) Give that "Tips List" away through your website, blog, and/or social media.

➤ Visit top article directories to search out articles by experts on a particular topic. Contact ten to twelve experts to gain permission to use their articles in an ebook. Of course you must give them full credit for their work. This can definitely work in your favor because they may be willing to help promote the final product.

➤ Write a list of the top ten questions you are most often asked about a particular problem you have a solution for. Record yourself asking the questions and giving the answers. Presto – an MP3 giveaway.

Boost Your Business While Generating Revenues

Creating an ethical bribe often results in a new product. Free products are just the tip of the iceberg for product creation. Developing information products will boost your business, your revenues, and your expert status more than just about anything else. There are information products used specifically for building your opt-in subscriber list, those that are used to generate revenue, and those that do both. In the next chapter you will learn exactly how to create products that sell.

Chapter 6

Create Information Products

One of the most rewarding elements of having an online business is the opportunity to communicate with men and women around the globe. There are a number of ways this can be done:

➤ Simple email messages
➤ Ezines
➤ Teleseminars
➤ Blogging
➤ Social marketing
➤ Information products – one of my personal favorites

Information products serve a number of purposes with some of the greatest benefits being building credibility, expert status, and revenues.

Ever since I created my first information product back in the mid-nineties, it's been so exciting to create something once and watch revenues come in more than once. It was in 2009 when I really understood the power of product creation; this is when everything in my life changed in an instant. My world had turned upside down with a single phone call and for the first time in fifteen-plus years of owning my business I chose to cancel several teleseminars, interviews, and client mentoring sessions and to postpone my various online events for an indefinite period of time. In a matter of four weeks I went from having two parents, a viable business, and not much that concerned me to my father passing away and me becoming one of the primary caretakers for my mother. I had no idea how long I would be caring for my mom, and I didn't much care. All I cared about was being able to answer a special calling *and* keeping my business running.

It didn't take long to recognize how important all the products I had created up to that point would be in generating revenue during this difficult time. I also recognized that as long as I had my computer and an Internet connection, I could continue to create products for my market.

Even when my mother fell ill and ended up in the hospital

for weeks and months on end, I was able to create products by her bedside. Had I not had this flexibility, one of two things would have occurred. One, my business would have suffered financially and my personal and professional responsibilities would have also suffered. Two, I could not have been there for my mother as much as I was able to be.

I directly attribute my ability to make the best choices for me and my family to having created several information products. I was not at the mercy of "dollars for hours."

If your business is not set up to give you the flexibility you choose and need, determine what information products you can create and take them to market as soon as possible. When your business is set up so that you are not trading dollars for hours 100 percent of the time, you have the flexibility you need to address unexpected situations and the freedom to make the choices in times of personal crisis or when you need to take time off. You can create this sustainability through multiple streams of revenue.

Information products are the best way to package your expertise and knowledge base. I know lots of people making hundreds, thousands, tens of thousands, and even hundreds of thousands of dollars each and every month with their information products. Many top experts offer everything from low-priced information products to high-priced resources.

Show Your Tribe That You Care

Regardless of what type of information products you create, do so with your end user in mind. Nothing comes through stronger than true concern for recipients of your information products. No matter what your industry, how long you have been doing what you do, or how much you generate in revenue, you never want to get so far removed from your readers that it appears as if you don't care.

This is especially true for markets targeted to people who

are going through a difficult period in their lives; they are more likely to be responsive if they know that you care about their needs and desires. By empathizing with them and showing that you know exactly what they are going through, you show that you are trustworthy. This should be easy for you to do, as you are an expert in the topic and you know a lot about the people in your niche. If you're not quite sure about what your market needs and wants, refer back to the chapter on surveys.

How Much; How Little?

Your financial and company goals determine how many products you offer. You may find one or two that best serve your client base, or perhaps dozens or even hundreds are appropriate. First find the answers to the following questions:

- What are the specific products you can provide?
- Do you offer a niche product or a wide variety of products?
- Can you clearly communicate the features and benefits of your products?
- Is the market for your products other businesses or will you market directly to consumers?

Before you decide to roll out new products, consider the development and marketing costs, the need for a clear vision of how to market them, and whether you have the necessary resources to introduce new products to your market.

Distribution

Who your market is and what their needs are determines how you will distribute your product. Distribution costs must be factored into your overhead costs and what you charge, and the distribution channel (method used to distribute) you choose impacts your marketing decisions. Distribution on the Internet is much more cost effective than traditional methods because you can use your own channel and those of joint-venture and affiliate partners.

Match the distribution channel you choose to your branding. Stay current with changes in the market so you can change your distribution channel as necessary. Consider:

→ Who will buy your product?
→ Is there a primary or secondary target market (a niche within a niche)?
→ What factors influence their decision to buy?
→ Who is involved in the purchase decision?
→ How often will they buy?
→ Where do they currently buy, when, and how much?
→ Is there opportunity to turn casual buyers into loyal buyers?
→ Can you build a long-term relationship with your market?

Other considerations
→ Is what you offer lucrative?
→ How will you reach your potential customers?

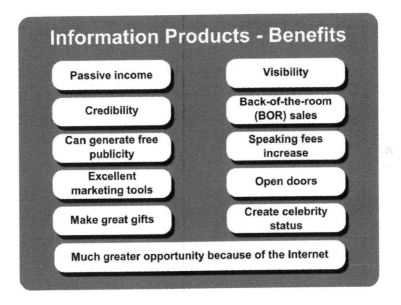

What Does Your Customer Want?
Throughout this book I urge you to "Pay attention to what your customers are asking for." Avoid developing your books, eb-

ooks, teleseminars, etc., in a vacuum if serving your market *and* making a profit is important to you.

The One-Product Wonder

Although you must start somewhere, your offerings and development should be ongoing processes in your business. This does not necessarily mean you need to be the person developing the products, but don't make the mistake of developing one product and never thinking about product development again. If you subscribe to this way of thinking you will either quickly be out of business or you will constantly struggle to generate revenues.

However, going to great lengths to develop a product without knowing whether or not it will sell can also cripple a business. Begin by introducing a very low-risk item such as an article, e-report, audio, or short ebook to test the waters. You can use a low-risk product as a springboard for others. And you can repurpose virtually anything you create.

My first product from 1995 was a cassette tape called *Living Life with Serenity*. What a laborious process it was to get that product to market! Creating information products in the nineties was very different, and much more difficult than it is today. In today's online arena, just about anyone can create a simple product such as an MP3 with a computer, a microphone, and editing software. Actually, you don't even need a microphone because a telephone works just fine with many software programs.

With print-on-demand technology you can send a master file to any one of hundreds of companies that create the product only as orders are received. And there's always the option of digitally downloaded products with extremely low production costs and very high profit margins.

Get More Mileage for Your Efforts

A great way to optimize your efforts is to package your information product in many different formats through what is referred to as *repurposing*. For example, you can write a report and repurpose it as a longer document and yet again as an ebook. Or your ebook can become a teleseminar. The teleseminar can become a mini-course. The mini-course can be turned into a mentoring program. And on and on.

When I was consulting with Dr. Joe Capista on his book *What Can a Dentist Teach You about Business, Life and Success?*, we immediately used the book content in a number of different ways. We turned portions into short articles. The articles were used to drive traffic to Dr. Capista's website and blog. The website offered a free ebook created from a chapter of the full book. At the end of the ebook we promoted the full book as well as Dr. Capista's speaking services. While we were still in development of the book, we arranged radio interviews and teleseminars. The calls were recorded and converted into MP3 files. The MP3 files were used to promote other products.

As you begin your product creation, think in terms of how you can stretch your efforts to fully serve your market while increasing your revenues and profit margins.

Product Lifecycle

The time a product is in existence, from start-up to close-out, is its lifecycle. The stages of a lifecycle include the idea stage, development, growth, maturity, decline, and close-out. Things that impact the life of a product are competition, increase or decrease in brand loyalty, emergence of alternative products, market saturation, and a downturn or upturn of the economy. Sales volume and profits are critical factors. And when a new method of online social marketing emerges, old methods may have run their course.

Some products have a seasonal cycle. For example, snow-shoes are more likely to sell during the winter months than in the summer. Swimsuits sell in spring and summer.

When a product is first introduced using traditional market-ing, sales are typically slow and profits minimal – if there are any profits at all. Many small business owners expect immediate profits, but that's not very realistic.

The Internet has changed how products go to market and how soon profits can be realized. You can quickly test the fea-sibility of a product marketed on the Internet with minimal in-vestment of money – if you have the necessary systems in place. And you can create great revenue and lots of new subscribers quickly.

In the growth stage – after your market has learned of your product's existence – both sales and profits rise at a rapid rate. But if you're not prepared for growth, your business can be overwhelmed. If you have more growth than you can handle, it can be as big a problem as no growth at all. Planning and hav-ing appropriate systems in place will help you prevent problems related to managing growth.

During the mature stage, even though sales may balance out, profits can increase. This is because the upfront investment of time, money, research, and development is behind you.

In the decline stage, both sales and profits decrease.

Being aware of the lifecycle process allows you to stay ahead of the curve and not make the mistake of holding on to a prod-uct line when you need to be creating something new or up-grading or changing the format of an existing product.

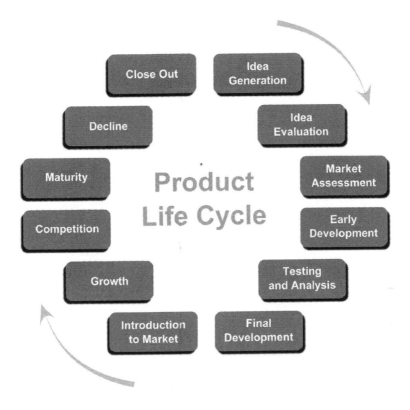

The Myth

Some people mistakenly presume that once a product is introduced to the market, it will always remain the same. This is not at all true. Look at the auto industry; although cars have been around for a long time, each year new models are introduced and go through a product lifecycle. Consumers have become more and more fickle, thereby making development a never-ending process. Even in the area of financial planning, as the market changes and the needs of that market change, mature products are abandoned and new products introduced.

Think about your product. Where is it in its lifecycle? How is the market impacting that cycle? What will need to happen to stay current with change?

Repurposing Online Information Products

As previously mentioned, with online information products you can repurpose your offerings quite easily, which keeps the lifecycle alive much, much longer. For example, you may have started with an ebook. It is likely that sales of the ebook will reach a peak and then decline. From there you can repurpose it into a teleseminar, then a full-day training, then a mentoring course, then workbooks, and then a redeveloped ebook. As the old saying goes, "You are only limited by your imagination" … and drive, and market need, and focus, and….

Recommend the Reader Become an Affiliate

If you've done a good job putting your e-product together, some of your customers might want to sell it to their market. Make this as easy as possible for them. I do this with many of my e-reports. As part of the content you can invite readers to become affiliates, provide a live link to where they can register, and move on to your next information product.

Links Page

Another way to monetize your information product is to include a links page with multiple recommendations. This is done on websites all the time. Why not include a full page or two in your e-report or ebook as well? I have a links page on my website with more of my own products and recommended products I sell as an affiliate. I often include affiliate links in my information product as well. With the products I am an affiliate for, I have used or read everything on my links pages, and only post links to products I am willing to stand behind.

When you are a top affiliate, you get noticed by high-visibility experts. I have been on the top-five and top-ten lists of many high-profile expert campaigns. This not only generates great revenues, it opens doors to more opportunities with expert partnerships. It goes beyond borrowed credibility; it is the "real deal" of your earning position and status. The more you can do this, the more influence you have. The more influence you have, the more you can get your message out to market.

There are any number of products you can sell by embedding links in an information product. Make sure there is a definite connection between the information product and what you are linking to.

Mini-Courses Attract Subscribers and Position Your Expertise

A mini-course is a short-term training program delivered at regular intervals – daily, weekly, or monthly. To gain fast interest from those who opt in for your mini-course, daily is a great choice. They are simple to create and are viewed as very high value by participants.

A mini-course is short- and long-term marketing at its best. One of my recent mini-courses generated more than 750 subscribers in a matter of weeks. Many of those who opted in went on to purchase a more in-depth training course. You can get the same result with a systemized approach to developing mini-courses.

You can develop a mini-course in a few hours. Let's say you've written a nonfiction how-to book. Use content directly from your book to create an online written training lesson or video and offer it to your subscribers. Every new subscriber is now a potential book buyer.

Here are the steps for getting your mini-course off the ground:

➻ Select the topic
➻ Divide it into subtopics
➻ Write the content
➻ Set up the lessons in your autoresponder program*
➻ Develop a landing page
➻ Market your mini-course

*An autoresponder program provides a number of email capabilities. There are several complete email marketing programs available that facilitate sending out mass newsletters, creating stylish opt-in forms, managing subscribers, segmenting your database, and more. Some of the more popular ones are Infusion-Soft®, 1ShoppingCart®, and AWeber.

Before investing in a program like one of these, review its capabilities to see if it will meet your needs. I am currently using InfusionSoft because it is quite robust. Automating your email marketing will save you time and, with the right program, you can maximize your efforts. When someone opts in for your mini-course, keep in touch so they won't forget about you.

I find the use of five lessons to be very effective for my mini-courses. You can have more or fewer lessons, but five gives you enough time to clearly establish your expertise and build trust with your market.

For each lesson, create a lesson number, the topic for that lesson, a statement about what the participant can expect from the next lesson, and a lead-in to a product you want to promote. Avoid giving too much away at no cost or people will expect everything you promote to be free. But make whatever information you give away highly valuable in order to build trust from your market. As you know, it can be very frustrating to opt in for something only to find that you wasted your time because the item is garbage. Talk about losing trust from the start. Don't let this happen to you.

Phase I and Phase II

There are two primary product phases to focus on. One is the development phase. The other is the sales and marketing phase. Be careful not to put the bulk of your focus on the development phase and very little on how to take the product to market – both are equally important.

Phases of Product Development

Always keep the big picture in mind and use one product to enhance another. As you are developing one product, determine how you could repackage that information in a way that continues to bring value to your market. Focusing only on development provides the illusion of productivity, often fooling us into believing that is what we need to do to grow our business. But without sales, your business won't last for long.

Start with a Low-Risk Product

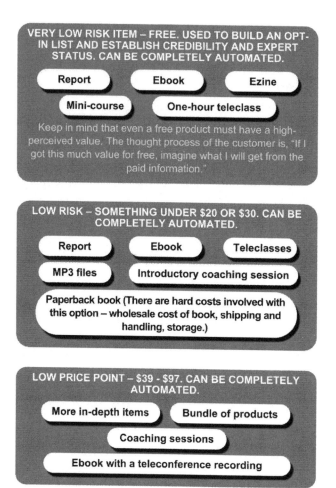

VERY LOW RISK ITEM – FREE. USED TO BUILD AN OPT-IN LIST AND ESTABLISH CREDIBILITY AND EXPERT STATUS. CAN BE COMPLETELY AUTOMATED.

- Report
- Ebook
- Ezine
- Mini-course
- One-hour teleclass

Keep in mind that even a free product must have a high-perceived value. The thought process of the customer is, "If I got this much value for free, imagine what I will get from the paid information."

LOW RISK – SOMETHING UNDER $20 OR $30. CAN BE COMPLETELY AUTOMATED.

- Report
- Ebook
- Teleclasses
- MP3 files
- Introductory coaching session
- Paperback book (There are hard costs involved with this option – wholesale cost of book, shipping and handling, storage.)

LOW PRICE POINT – $39 - $97. CAN BE COMPLETELY AUTOMATED.

- More in-depth items
- Bundle of products
- Coaching sessions
- Ebook with a teleconference recording

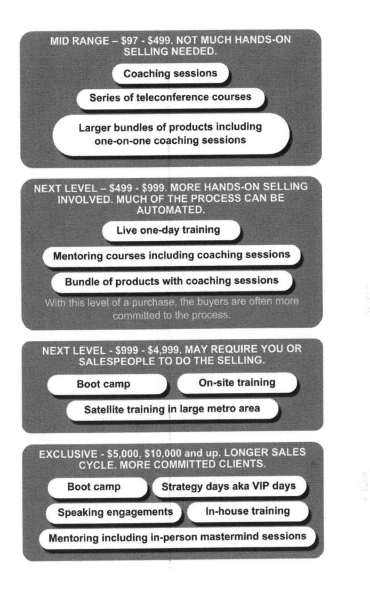

The Process in Action

When my colleague Lori Giovannoni wanted to gain an online presence and build her opt-in subscriber list, we needed to come up with something that was easy to create yet had high value for her market. Lori had been a professional speaker for over twenty-five years and had coached numerous emerging speakers, taught courses on professional speaking, and mentored many professional speakers.

To begin her online presence, we went into action to create a simple ebook that took very little time to develop. We called it *So You Want to Be a Professional Speaker?*

Here is an overview of what we did.

➤ Lori wanted to increase her market reach to those interested in the profession of speaking.

➤ We decided on a short and simple ebook of no more than fifteen to twenty pages.

➤ We determined market need. That wasn't too difficult because both Lori and I have been professional speakers for years.

➤ Lori decided on the main topic and listed others that most speakers want more information about.

➤ She wrote one to five paragraphs for each area of interest.

➤ We formatted the ebook, designed a simple cover, and made it into a PDF file.

➤ We used the ebook to build an opt-in list, which increased by several hundred in a few weeks.

Because of the focus of the ebook, those who opted in were very warm leads for her next offering, a four-week group coaching teleclass, and Lori secured a few private clients from the teleclass. The process is actually very simple and just about anyone can do it as long as they get into action.

If you have not yet gotten in the game of product creation, now is the time. With each day that passes you are literally leaving money on the table. When you implement the information in this chapter, you could feasibly get an information product to market in as little as forty-eight hours.

Chapter 7

The Power of
a Responsive List

There's Gold in Them Thar Hills!

You have likely heard "The gold is in the list." Actually, a more accurate statement is "The gold is in the *quality* of your list." Don't put off building a responsive opt-in subscriber list. It's amazing how often someone can hear that they need to build a list and yet it goes to the bottom of their priority list. It actually needs to be at the top. Imagine that you have a hungry market that is ready to buy anything you offer – a market of raving fans who tell others about how wonderful your information is – a tribe of people you love serving. Without a list, your road to success will be a steep uphill climb.

If you do just one thing each day to build your list, you will be amazed at the potential for revenues you can create. Doing more increases your chance of success. Stop procrastinating and get over whatever fear is holding you back from building your list. Realize that you are here to serve your market and that when you build your list you will be able to more fully serve those who *want* what you have to offer.

No more excuses. Build your list now!

Where to Start

An opt-in list is a list of email addresses of people who have agreed to receive information from you via email. This is known as *permission marketing*. If you send them commercial email messages without that permission, you are spamming them, and spamming is against the law. When you have permission from those you are sending messages to, you are not spamming them. To learn more about this law, do a Google search on "Can Spam Laws." To get the correct information, go to the Federal Trade Commission (FTC) website.

You must always give those you contact the option to unsubscribe whenever they want to. When you use a reputable service provider like AWeber, 1ShoppingCart®, GetResponse, or InfusionSoft®, this obligation is built in to your system.

To minimize opt-outs, it's essential to offer high-value information that encourages people to stay on your list. A good rule of thumb is to include three high-value messages with every sales message you send.

The format of the value-added messages depends on your market. At a minimum you can send text email messages, HTML, or a series of videos. I find that direct-to-camera videos build trust faster. Direct-to-camera videos are videos in which you are in front of the camera and it is you people see rather than a screen shot of what you are teaching.

The Two-Second Rule

There is so much noise people have to wade through online that it is imperative that you quickly catch their attention. The Two-Second Rule means you have two seconds to grab a visitor's attention. Although it is called the Two-Second Rule, you often have *less than two seconds* in which to do this.

To increase your conversion rate, make sure your material is very easy to read, jumps out at people, and is all about building your list. Keep things clear and simple.

Take a look at the opt-in box above. It is visible, easy to read, and the wording immediately draws your attention. There is no confusion about what you need to do.

Convey some type of benefit to your visitor to encourage them to opt in. Whatever you offer, the goal should be to get people to your website, blog, or landing page in order to download something. If the download item is free, they are more likely to leave their contact information.

Initially you should request minimal information such as name and email address. The more contact information you ask for, the more likely a new visitor will click out of your site without leaving any information; you have not yet gained their trust.

Once you have name recognition and people know and trust you, they will opt in. Put consistent effort into gaining visibility and trust to gain the long-term benefits of a subscriber list.

Make Money at the Press of a Button

When you have a responsive subscriber list, you can literally make money at the press of a button. Once you see what your list can do for you, you will likely make it a priority. I have been known to make thousands of dollars in a day (sometimes tens of thousands), and so have many of my colleagues, due to the quality of our lists. If you're serious about making great money, now is the time to make list-building a part of your everyday business practice.

Caution: Some Designers Resist the Opt-In

Some web designers don't have a marketing mindset, and may resist putting an opt-in box on your website, blog, or landing page. Don't let them make this decision for you. An opt-in box is extremely important for all the reasons discussed above. More and more web designers understand the marketing mindset, but yours might tell you that it doesn't "look good."

During a recent coaching session with a client, we talked about a challenge she was having with one of her new customers who refused to have an opt-in box on her main page, choosing rather to immediately try to sell people on a product that was not widely recognized. My client was afraid she would lose her customer if she got too insistent on the opt-in box. I told her it was her responsibility to recommend what she knows will work and not to worry about upsetting her client. It's better to rock the boat in order for your clients to get a result than to "play nice" and they get no result at all. Clients don't hire you to tell them everything they want to hear. Well, I stand corrected – there may be people out there like that, but are they who you want to work with? I would venture to say no.

A rule of thumb in being a conscious entrepreneur is that there will be times you have to make tough calls that are in the best interest of your customer. They may not immediately understand or agree with what you are recommending, but if you know it is in their best interest, defend your position even if you risk losing your customer; you will surely lose them if you back down from the right recommendation.

Stand your ground if it is really the right thing to do. Regardless of whether it's with your designer or a client, stay focused on why a list is so important.

With your designer you can say, "I want an opt-in box because that's how I'm going to build my list." It's one of the most important business decisions you will make. Don't put it off or you will be saying, "I wish I had done this months (even years) ago. Imagine if I had captured three people a day during that time. What would that have done for me by now?"

With your clients, always think in terms of what is really in their best interest. Call it as you see it based on this perspective.

In recent years there have been a number of templates designed for opt-in pages that convert very nicely. WordPress has a theme called OptimizePress that converts very nicely. I've used it dozens of times with great results. Check it out.

There are many choices today for templates that take a lot of the guesswork out of developing landing pages. In many cases, the cost is considerably less than hiring a designer.

Be a Resource before Being a Vendor

Most people have grown accustomed to getting lots of free information, much of which is of little value to them. To gain trust and respect from your subscribers, go above and beyond what others are doing. They will view you as a valuable resource if you provide incredibly high-value information and position yourself as an expert. Then when it comes time to offer something for sale, it will be easy for them to "click here now."

The first step is to have something people *want* to opt in for. Whether it's an ebook, MP3, report, white paper, video, or live teleseminar, it should be of interest to your market and offer a solution to a problem they have. The more you know about your market, the more likely you will be able to provide a solution they are interested in. Here are four simple ways to determine what to offer:

- Surveys
- Market specific forums
- Media trends
- Discussions in social media

The more you know, the more targeted your approach to development and delivery of your product can be, which equates to higher revenues and higher profit margins.

Automation Is the Name of the Game

Although you can capture potential subscribers' contact information manually (which is a huge mistake), you really should automate it using a reliable program. There are a number of different service providers for building your subscriber list. You can choose a basic program or a very elaborate system. Costs range from a few dollars a month to hundreds, even thousands. For someone just starting out, the most robust program is likely not a great investment. However, you should think in terms of where you want your business to be rather than where it currently is.

Building Your List

As mentioned previously, there are those who really do make money at the press of a button. Many experts claim you can make hundreds, thousands, tens of thousands, and even hundreds of thousands of dollars. Is this true? Absolutely! On many occasions I have made thousands within a day or two of sending out an email message by just pressing the send button.

But make no mistake about it – this didn't happen overnight. To believe otherwise is to set yourself up for a huge letdown.

The only way to make money at the press of a button is to lay a solid foundation and build your opt-in subscriber list on an ongoing basis. If you want secure revenue streams, you should be constantly building your list. This is where funnel marketing comes in. Start with something that's easy to create and implement, and grow from there. You'll need more than one way for people to get on your list, and there are effective and ineffective ways to build a list.

Ineffective List-Building

Don't get stuck on these ineffective methods:

➻ Buying lists – Buying a list is exactly as it sounds. You purchase a list that you hope will be valuable. Yet in many cases buying a list not very effective unless it is very, very targeted. A targeted list can be a very wise investment with a high return for you investment. But an extremely targeted list is very costly.

➻ Massive blasts from a service you pay – not effective. There are services that mail to untold numbers of people without targeting. Rather than building your list you're more likely to irritate the end user and lose them as a potential client.

➤ Taking email addresses off of websites and adding them to your subscriber list without permission. This is spamming and is against the law.

➤ Opting in to an expert's list and adding the expert's name to your list without permission from them. This is not only considered spamming, but we all know that it is very annoying to receive unrequested information. Just because you have an interest in their information does not mean they have an interest in yours. Imagine if everyone who signed up for their information did this. Not good!

Some time ago I received a message from a woman who was very annoyed that I had not requested to get on her email distribution list. I had no idea what she was talking about. Apparently, at a live event I hosted, she asked if I wanted to be put on her list. She never explained what she did, why it would benefit me, or what I would receive from her. Besides that, I was so focused on doing a great job at the event that it was not the best time to ask me about getting on her list. Several months had passed when I received her message, and all that time she had resented that I wasn't on her list.

I was floored. For her to put that much energy into one person getting on her list to the detriment of building it with people who really wanted to be on it was ridiculous. Her logic was, "If someone comes on my list I am always going to go on theirs." Turns out she had about fifty people on her list. My response to her was, "What about when you have thousands of people on your list. Not only will it not be possible for you to keep up with emails from all those people, you likely won't have an interest in many of them." I told her that for her to assume everyone should be on her list was a huge mistake. Not sure how she would respond to my direct approach, I let it go – that is, until I got a message a few days later thanking me for my guidance. She said that after giving thought to what I told her, she realized she had been setting unrealistic expectations of others.

The point of this story is that you are better off focusing on building your list with people who *want* to be on your list. Quality is far more important than quantity. Focus on people who really want your information and you will be light years ahead of those who focus solely on list size.

Effective List-Building

- ➡ Opt-in box on your website or blog
- ➡ Landing pages with special offers
- ➡ Signature (sig) file at the end of your email messages
- ➡ Opt-in box on various social network sites you belong to
- ➡ Resource box at the end of an article
- ➡ Blogging with a link leading to an opt-in box
- ➡ Signature file on forum postings where permissible
- ➡ Media releases announcing a giveaway
- ➡ Teleseminars and webinars that participants must opt in for
- ➡ Live presentations
- ➡ Paid advertising in targeted publications and on targeted sites and social networks
- ➡ Affiliate partnerships
- ➡ Interviews in which your website, blog, or landing page is announced

Hot Tip: Make sure you have an opt-in box on every page of your blog and website.

In the past, inviting people to sign up for an ezine (online newsletter) was a great way to build an opt-in list. It was as simple as adding "Get our Newsletter," and people would opt in. Not so anymore. With all the choices people have today, without conveying the specific benefits of your product to potential subscribers, an ezine likely won't have much appeal. High-value *free* offers include:

- E-reports
- Teleseminars and webinars
- Expert interviews
- Ebooks
- White papers
- Chapters of your book
- MP3s

Super List-Building Strategies

Social Networks

Facebook, LinkedIn, Google+, Pinterest, Ning, Twitter, and other online social networks have become an integrated part of the Internet. Some people miss that *social* is the vital idea behind social networks – it's not *sell, sell, sell.* To get the most out of your efforts, contribute to the social aspect of your networks and make your offers for opt-in only periodically.

Put a message about your offer on your profile page and stagger additional offers across the networks you use. Check the help section or FAQ section of each social network to find out what you can and cannot do. Be sure to pay very close attention to the rules because you can get kicked out of a social network for no apparent reason.

Forums

Forums are a great way to build your list. An Internet forum, or message board, is an online discussion site where people can hold conversations in the form of posted messages. Each forum has its own set of rules, so be sure to check the rules and guidelines for those you choose to join.

Forums are a great place to connect with people who have similar interests. I've belonged to health and nutrition forums, boxer dog forums, and Internet marketing forums. When my father was diagnosed with brain and lung cancer, I found a forum specific to the exact type of lung cancer my father had. Finding a group of people who had something as devastating as that in common was incredible.

In some cases it is not appropriate to promote anything on a forum, while in other cases it is. The cancer forum was not at all the place to promote, while the one for online marketing definitely was.

The way to get the greatest return on your investment of time and effort is to get involved in discussions and contribute high-value information. Avoid joining simply to promote your product. Be transparent and let people get to know you for who you truly are. Forums are meant to be interactive; they are not for self-promotion.

Find forums specific to your market. Be an active participant who is known for your contribution rather than for trying to build your list or make a sale. To find a forum, go to http://www.google.com and search for "Forums + [your topic]." For example, if you're looking for a forum for owners of boxer dogs, search for "Forums + Boxer Dogs."

A very subtle way to attract subscribers is to develop a signature (sig) file that offers something of high value. A sig file is a very small text file that takes people to your landing page and can be automatically attached to the end of emails, articles, forum postings, etc. When used with articles, a sig file may be referred to as a *resource box*. Not all forums allow you to add a sig file or resource box to your posts, so be sure to check the rules. If it is allowed, it is a great way to offer something of value and get people to your landing page.

Example #1: The sig file below is more about me than benefits to the potential subscriber. Results may not be optimal.

> Example One
>
> Kathleen Gage works with consciously aware speakers, authors, coaches and consultants who are ready to turn their knowledge into money-making products and services. She does this by teaching them how to publish their works via books, eBased information products, teleseminars, webinars and any medium that can be distributed via the Internet.
> Get her FREE video - Marketing 101 - www.PowerUpForProfits.com

Example #2: Below is a "results driven" sig file. It's likely to get a much better response than Example #1, especially when used in a forum filled with people who have an interest in making money with teleseminars. To use the sig file below in a health and nutrition forum is not a good match. Again, make sure your message, your market, and your offer are aligned.

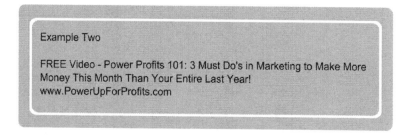

> Example Two
>
> FREE Video - Power Profits 101: 3 Must Do's in Marketing to Make More Money This Month Than Your Entire Last Year!
> www.PowerUpForProfits.com

Dozens of Methods to Choose From

As you've read, there are dozens upon dozens of ways to gain visibility, build your subscriber list, and position your expertise. The more visible you are, the better. To get your message out in a big way, be consistent in what you do to gain visibility.

Start Building Your List Now

Answer this fast… what's your number one list-building strategy?

If you answered, "I don't know," please make list-building a priority. The world of online marketing has changed since the onslaught of social media marketing, and some people are under the mistaken belief that if they are very involved in social media they don't need an opt-in subscriber list. But nothing could be further from the truth. Virtually any business in any industry can benefit from a subscriber list.

What's fabulous about online marketing is you can put systems in place that allow you to build your list 24/7. Article marketing, automated webinars, and advertising can all run 24/7.

Imagine what could change for your marketing if you had a list of people who purchased each and every time you sold something. I'm not saying every person on your list will buy from you again, but even if only a portion of them are repeat customers, you can make a great living. In addition you can literally start a movement, shift perceptions, and make lasting changes.

The way of the world has changed for many of us. It used to be you needed lots of money to start a movement. Today you can do incredible things with very little money if need be. The more you understand and use the Internet, the more impact you can have. The more you focus on building a community, the more impact you can have. The more you honor what your mission is, the more impact you can have.

And you don't have to build your list all on your own. With the right partnerships, others help you build your list. And with effective list-building strategies in place, you can work less and make more.

How do you do it? You've likely heard of OPM. To most people it means "other people's money." In the context of list-building it means "other people's markets." By tapping in to the potential of other people marketing for you, you gain greater market reach. By having your own personal sales and marketing team that is eager to tell others about your product, you increase your earning potential. Not only will you increase revenues, but you will also increase your impact on those you are meant to make a difference to. I think most people would agree that this is a great way to build your business.

Ask *any* successful person who uses the Internet to market what their number one source of traffic is, and in many cases they'll tell you it's their joint-venture (JV) and affiliate partnerships and programs. And as you've read, JV and affiliate marketing are not the only ways to build a list; they are just two among many. I discuss JV and affiliate partnerships in more detail in Chapter 15.

Here's a surefire way to succeed at list-building: Every day for a week, implement one list-building strategy from this book. The following week add one more strategy. The following week add one more strategy. Repeat this for several weeks, and before you know it you will have created ample ways to build your list. Remember, it doesn't have to be you doing the work. If you have a support person, they can do the heavy lifting.

Having a great subscriber list is your ticket to impacting a great many people on a regular basis and earning the kind of income you dream of earning. It can literally recession-proof your business. While others are struggling, you can make offers at various price points that will appeal to your subscribers.

It doesn't matter whether your business is online or offline, having your own list of customers and prospective customers means that you can get them to visit your store, website, blog, landing page, or sales page practically on command. This ability to drive traffic on command can keep your income steady through good times and the not-so-good times. Of course, repeat business is based on your customer's initial experience; if it's not a good one, they won't be back. And they will opt out of your list.

But when someone has a great experience with you and feels their time was well invested, they will be back again and again and again. Here are ten tips for list-building:

#1 – Build a Solid Foundation for Your Business

A list is something that *you* control at all times. You control when you send information to your subscribers, whether or not you continue to grow your list, what your relationship with subscribers will be, and even how often you make offers. A quality list is a solid foundation for your business and one of your most important business assets. If you decide to sell your business, the quality of your list determines the value of your business to a potential buyer.

#2 – Understand That People Are More Likely to Buy from Those They Trust

It's getting more and more difficult for new businesses to find customers. Some people simply will not buy from those they've never heard of and with whom they don't have a relationship. You usually have to "pre-sell" before someone will make a purchase. One of the main ways to do this is to offer an ethical bribe; people are likely to join your list because they view providing their email address as a lower risk than making a purchase. This gives you the opportunity to gain their trust and build a relationship that can lead to a sale down the road.

Another pre-sell method is a third-party endorsement from an affiliate or joint-venture partner. My point is that people have to feel very safe with those with whom they are dealing.

#3 – A One-Time Customer Can Turn into a Lifetime Customer

The difference between customers who buy from you one time and those who buy from you multiple times is often the amount of communication they receive after their initial transaction. It is also a matter of how much they like and trust you. The better the communication and the more valuable the communication, the more likely they are to trust and like you.

Even if a customer had a great experience with you, you are likely to fall to the back of their mind if they don't hear from you for a while. If they receive follow-up emails from you, it's an entirely different matter. You'll be on their mind and you'll likely create a lifetime customer.

Implement a system of ongoing follow-up notices to your customers. If you don't, you'll be out of sight and out of mind. There are many other "experts" out there who are vying for *your* customer's attention, and if you are not conscientious about your communication, they'll get the customer that you once had.

#4 – It's Easier to Sell to a Previous Customer

This point goes hand in hand with the previous one. If you spend all your time chasing new customers, your profits are going to be far less than if you focus on keeping old customers happy and selling to them over and over again. If you don't have additional products to sell to your customers, send affiliate promotions for products of value to your market.

#5 – Use List-Building to Grow Your Income

When you have a list, you can get people to look at your special offers and new products whenever you'd like. All it takes is a simple email and you can literally make money with the press of a button. The key is consistency.

#6 – Don't Buy Leads

When I started out on the Internet many years ago, I was very tempted to buy lists of thousands of email addresses. What was true then is true now: In the majority of cases buying leads doesn't work. There's always an exception to the rule, but for the most part you are better off building your list through focused efforts.

If you do buy a list, there's a good chance you won't have a very responsive list. People are more likely to consider what you send them as an intrusion and immediately delete your messages. Think about when you get junk email from someone you don't know. Not only do you delete the message, you are likely to block the address, report them as a spammer, and immediately get off their list. Don't be one of these annoying marketers.

When you build your own list from scratch (organically), you're contacting people who have warmed up to you already and who are a lot more likely to buy your product. Buying leads, for the most part, is a waste of money. There are, however, occasions when paid advertising can be very effective. Targeted trade journals, specific social networks such as Facebook, and paid ads on a targeted blog can all be good uses of your advertising dollars.

Whichever way you go, analyze your results to see what kind of traffic the ad generated and what the conversion to sales was. You have to analyze your results if your list is going to work for you, whether it's an organic list or from paid advertising.

#7 – Don't Spam People!

It is awfully enticing to hear that all you need to do to make money is send an email. It can lead you to believe that everyone wants to hear from you and will buy what you offer. But as pointed out in tip #6 above, unwelcome email gets you nowhere. What you are really doing is spamming. DON'T! STOP! HALT!

Spamming is when you send unsolicited emails, and it is actually against the law. The spam law states that people should have requested your email in some way, such as opting in to your list, and that you must make it easy for people to unsubscribe from your list (a link at the bottom of the message is best). You are also required by law to include your postal address in all emails you send. Note that I said postal address and not home address. If need be, get a post office box for your online correspondence.

Building a relationship may take longer than spamming, but the profits are far greater in the long run.

#8 – Don't Put Off Building a List

Hopefully I am getting this point across – **don't put off building your list.** You might think you can put it off until you are more established, or until you have reached some other goal, but putting off list-building is a huge mistake. Even if your traffic is low and you're new to online business, now is the time to build those relationships.

If you ask established online entrepreneurs what their biggest regret is, many of them will tell you it's that they did not start building their list sooner. It doesn't matter what your online business is – selling books, information products, teleseminars, ebooks, offering a service, affiliate marketing, ecommerce, blogging, or direct selling – you need to build a list right from the start.

#9 – Build Relationships First; Focus on Money Later

Before you focus on making money, build relationships with others. If all you do is sell, sell, sell, you're risking ticking people off and gaining a lot of unsubscribers. People opt in to your list for a reason: to get something of value from you. A constant sales pitch is not something of value. Whether it's an e-course, a free ebook, an information product, coupons, notices, an audio, or something else, they expect to receive a lot of value for being on your email list. If you provide this relationship first, the money will follow – that is if you have something to sell.

On more occasions than I can recall I asked someone who was complaining about not making money what they were selling, and they answered that they weren't selling anything. Really?! I have to wonder what they're thinking. How do they expect to make money if they don't offer something for sale? As farfetched as this sounds, it has happened not only to me but to many of my colleagues – people complaining about not making money but they honestly have nothing to sell. To make money you do have to have something to sell.

#10 – Be Consistent

Avoid another common mistake – building a list and then doing nothing with it. Arghhhh. This is as bad as not building a list.

Not keeping in touch makes people forget you. No matter how memorable you think you are, most people have so much going on that they don't remember many of the things they opt in for. Help them remember by keeping in touch.

One of the first places I often have my clients make changes is in how often they communicate with their subscribers and what they send. Several of my clients hadn't corresponded with their list for over a year. After clarifying what their purpose was, what their goals were, and what they wanted to accomplish with their market, I had them send out emails to establish their new position.

One client had what she thought was a list of 8,000 subscribers. Although the number read 8,000, the reality was that the list was substantially smaller. After over a year of not communicating, she sent an email inviting her current subscribers to opt in for another list. The result was shocking. It turned out that only 200 of the 8,000 were interested in the change. What this meant was that she had to start from scratch to rebuild her list.

But not all was lost. It simply meant she needed to get into action – fast! With one strategy that included bringing a new product to market, not only did she build her list by nearly 5,000, she generated over $35,000. Now she stays in close contact with her subscribers and continues to offer some amazing products to them.

Another client was making a huge change in her business. She was going from a very conservative market to one that was interested in metaphysical topics. I recommended that she send out a message with the subject line *I've been keeping something from you,* which sparked subscribers' curiosity. The body of the message addressed some important changes that were being made in her business and offerings. I warned her that she would likely have quite a few opt-outs due to the change in her vision and direction. Sure enough, she did. And yet she found a whole new group of people who are incredibly interested in what she is currently doing.

If you have not been in touch for some time or you make a major shift in what you are doing, realize that not everyone will be as excited about your new direction as you are. But it's very likely there will be some who have been waiting for a change and they will come along for the ride with renewed interest.

The more authentic you are, the more you will attract those who really love what you do, offer, and stand for.

Keep the Long-Term Results in Mind

One of the most important things you can do as a list owner is to have empathy for your subscribers. In other words, don't abuse them. If you've subscribed to lists yourself, you might have noticed that people sometimes "use" their list members. This upsets and frustrates them, and they will likely opt out.

The same thing can happen with people who join your list. Before you send your message, think about the long-term effects it could have. If you're just trying to make a quick buck and you're not promoting quality, it will come back to bite you in the end.

Affiliates and List-Building

As you gain more visibility and build a responsive list, others will want you to promote their information through your list. Without realizing it you can agree to do far more mailings for others than is in the best interests of your subscribers. Do your homework before agreeing to send out messages on behalf of others, whether they are joint-venture or affiliate partners or not. Create a promotions calendar and map out a period of six to twelve months to determine if there are overlaps in what you are doing.

January

			1	2	3	4
5	6	7	8	9	10	11
12	13	14	15	16	17	18
19	20	21	22	23	24	25
26	27	28	29	30	31	

January	Kick off the year with special product launch
February	Affiliate - Mary Stuberg's product
March	Blog tour - 10 blogs to write articles for
April	Teleseminars on marketing / Affiliate - Susan Browning
May	Hosted webinars with Susan Browning, Mary Stuberg, Debra Joneston
June	Affiliate launch for Lynn Dreamston
July	Virtual book tour
August	Hosted webinars with Nancy Bryce, Janet Broomston, Mike Jones
September	New product launch
October	Live event
November	Telesummit
December	End of year sale

As an affiliate, it's a good idea to review the products that you're promoting to make sure they are high quality. Don't promote something just because there is a high commission for you! Always think in terms of how the product will benefit your market, and always make sure it is a good fit for those you are promoting to.

The more other experts know, like, and trust you, the more opportunities open up. For example, someone who has been around for a while and has a great reputation is often invited to review products they can sell.

If you are fairly new to the affiliate arena, you may have to purchase something before you reach a point at which someone will give you a product to review. As you become known to other experts, they will often invite you to look at their product before you make a decision. When someone approaches you to sell their information product, they should be willing to give it to you for review without your having to purchase it. If they are not willing to give you a review copy, you may not want to promote it. After all, why would you promote something blindly? Again, this is when they approach you.

On the flip side, if you approach someone to promote their product, you will likely have to purchase it first. They might think you simply want a free item and don't intend to consider being an affiliate. The more well-known you are, the more inclined others will be to provide a product for your review. This is why you want to do all you can, at all times, to gain market position and visibility.

The same thing applies if you sell tangible products. Make sure that everything you do and the products you promote are in the best interest of your subscribers. I have been involved in a number of online book launches for hardcopy books. Before I promote one, I need to see the physical book to get a really good sense if it is the kind and quality of book I want to introduce to my market.

I have to laugh when someone asks me to promote their book and then hesitates to provide a copy or tells me they will send me the ebook version to save themselves money. If I am going to promote a book, I want to get a good "feel" for it. I turn down about 95 percent of these requests either because the book is not a good match for my market, the quality is not the best, or I don't want to overwhelm my subscribers with too many promotional messages.

In Conclusion

Building your list can be a fun and profitable experience. Use the dos and don'ts above, and you will have a much tighter and more responsive list.

Chapter 8

Blogging for Fame and Fortune

If you've been online for any length of time, it's likely you've heard that you should blog. But exactly what that means is open to interpretation.

Let's start with defining what a blog is. A blog is a type of website, or web log, where you regularly post *entries*, also known as *posts* – informative commentaries, articles, promotional information, graphics, MP3s, and/or videos. Posts are usually listed in reverse chronological order.

The word *blog* can also be used as a verb meaning "to post on your blog." Blogging is a great way to build your list. With effective blogging you can direct readers to your website or landing page where they can opt in for something free (an ethical bribe). You can also effectively establish your "voice" if you're willing to let your personality shine through on your posts.

To get the most out of your blog, post consistently on a regular basis – a minimum of two to three times a week, and more if possible – using fresh content containing market-related keywords for the search engines. By using targeted keywords you increase the right kind of traffic to your blog.

Many people have blogs, but some are more of an embarrassment than a business-building tool. If your blog looks like it was designed by an amateur, with blurring images, content all over the place, too many font sizes and colors, and there is no branding to speak of, you're wasting your time if you expect it to enhance your business. If you offer great content on your blog, you will get visitors. If you include your sig file, readers will opt in to your list. And if you include a rich site summary (RSS) feed, they can subscribe to receive an update every time you post to your blog.

Check out the RSS feeds offered by www.feedburner.com and www.feedblitz.com. You can get the free version of both, or you can invest a few dollars a month and you won't have to put up with the advertising they send when you register for the free service.

When I first heard about RSS feeds many years ago, I about drove myself crazy trying to understand the mechanics of how they worked. I wasted a lot of time learning about the technology before realizing that I don't need to understand how they work; I just need to know that they *do* work for keeping my fresh content in front of interested readers.

The beauty of using an RSS feed service is that it's yet another opt-in list you can market to. When you post to your blog content that promotes something, it feeds out to your blog subscribers.

Another way to build your list through your blog is to add an opt-in box "above the fold" – the area visible without scrolling down (also referred to as "above the scroll"). Always be sure your opt-in opportunity is prominently positioned.

Let's assume you are a nutritionist who teaches clients how to keep their weight under control. Rather than captioning your offer "Sign up for my ezine" and hoping people will opt in, try something timely like "7 Ways to LOSE Weight During the Holiday Season" to get a higher conversion rate. Change it up when the holiday season is over.

Another way to grow your subscriber list is to end your posts with a link to your landing page where they will find a free offer. Visit www.themarketingmindset.com to view my marketing blog. Be sure to opt in to the FeedBlitz RSS feed on the right-hand side. The opt-in is in the box that reads "*Stay On Top of All the Tips, Strategies and Insights – Subscribe to The Marketing Mindset Blog.*"

Setting Up a Blog

There are plenty of vendors who will be happy to set up your blog, so if you're not too tech-savvy, do yourself a favor and hire someone to do it. I did. I learned a long time ago that it is more cost effective to hire out the jobs I have no business doing myself.

Even though I will not be teaching you to the mechanics of setting up a blog, I recommend that you use the WordPress platform. This is a program you use to write blog entries instead of Word or some other word processing program. It's what I use, and I love it. Check out my blog at www.TheMarketingMindset. com

Why You Need to Have a Blog

It is very difficult to optimize your online presence without a blog in the mix. Following are some of the primary reasons.

Be Viewed as an Expert

One of the best uses for a blog is to establish your credibility and expert status. Keep in mind that eyeballs will read your information and judge you on the quality of your content. Be sure it's worth reading and keep it relevant and of interest to your readers.

People read blogs not only for the information but also for enjoyment and because they are interested in the blogger, so don't shy away from adding your personality to your posts. Think about the blogs you most enjoy reading. What is it about them you enjoy? What keeps you going back for more?

Showcase Yourself

Those who sign up for your subscriber list want to learn more about you and your product. They would not sign up if they weren't sure they could learn valuable information or gain some insights. That's why you should present yourself as an expert at all times. Does this mean you can't have a sense of humor? Absolutely not! If that's your personality, go for it. But don't waste people's time with unproductive jokes and comics. They will soon grow weary of them.

People trust and look up to experts. Your relationship with your subscribers will grow stronger than ever as you share your expert strategies, tips, and tricks to help them. Avoid overloading people with every little thing in which you are featured. This is counterproductive.

Show Your Subscribers Real Results or Data

If you can offer case studies or data, you will get great results by sharing these things with your subscribers. For example, if you are an expert at selling books via Amazon.com, you can provide real-life case studies of what you have done. Or if you are an expert at selling low-priced reports, you can show people how you write reports, price them, and get the most out of each sale.

This works across many different types of businesses. The point is that people like to see real-time results, and they are often impressed by and respond to them. This works very well when you have used a product that you are eventually going to promote. You can also recommend third-party resources for data about products you're promoting.

Media Relations

It is not uncommon for the media to find a story of interest in a blog posting. If you get an inquiry from the media, be quick to respond. You can also use your blog for crisis management. Let's say you work with a high-profile client and something negative about them makes its way into the media. You or your client can respond immediately by way of a blog posting, and it will hit the web immediately. This is not a common need for solopreneurs or small businesses, but it's ideal in some situations.

Customer Relations

Blogs are an excellent way to keep in touch with customers, announce new products, feature a company you work with, host industry experts, and keep customers informed about changes in their industries.

Voice an Opinion

Have an opinion on something? Your blog is a great way to express your opinion, especially since you can write virtually anything you want to. What better way to let people know what you think and value? Blogs have provided a greater change in how we position our expertise than just about anything in the last few decades. With blogs and social media you can create a persona that attracts a specific following.

Host Guest Bloggers

As an expert, be on the lookout for as many ways to raise market awareness, credibility, and status as you can possibly find. A great way to do this is to host high-profile experts to contribute to your blog. This is an incredible way to spike your credibility and the popularity of your blog.

Invite experts your readers want to hear from, and make sure you convey the benefit to the expert. The more visible someone is, the more they are approached for all sorts of reasons. Some have "gatekeepers" who filter through the many requests they get.

When you invite an expert to post on your blog, be prepared with information such as what your blog is about, who your readers are, how many subscribers you have (if the number is substantial), how you intend to promote their post, what you would like them to blog about, and when you need the post. In some cases *they* will let *you* know what they will and will not write about and when they can get the information to you.

Guest bloggers often promote their post to *their* readers as well, and they might tweet about their post. This is a major benefit to you.

Think through your promotional plan for letting people know you have a high-profile guest blogger, and gain as much leverage from the post as possible.

A few creative marketers have taken the idea of expert contributors to a very high level. My colleagues and friends, Denise Wakeman and Ellen Britt, came up with an idea that took the online marketing world by storm. They secured a group of dozens of experts to be regular contributors. We all agreed to submit one article per month, that we would do no promoting or selling, and that we would help promote their blog called The Future of Ink. From the very first article release, the idea was a hit. Not only did lots and lots of traffic come to the blog, but the comments and feedback were beyond compare. One reason it worked so well was that having no promoting or selling enhanced the blog's integrity; it was high-value information only. Another reason is that Denise and Ellen were extremely well organized. They made it very clear to the experts they approached that this was an exclusive opportunity and that they had been handpicked to participate. If you can convey the benefits of posting to your site, you will get a more positive response from the experts you approach.

The right combination of your content and content from experts will drive traffic to your blog.

Can you see why it's essential to make your blog "visitor ready"? To get that great traffic to your blog and then have no way for them to opt in to your list would truly be a shame.

Survey Your Market

Posting a survey on your blog is a great way to find out something about your market fast. If you haven't focused on building a following on your blog, it will likely sit dormant. But if you've built a strong following, you are likely to get a good response from your survey.

You can also post your *permalink* – a URL that permanently links to your blog or other item – with the survey on Twitter, Facebook, YouTube, LinkedIn, and all other social media networks you are involved with to create more leverage.

Product Reviews

Blogs are an excellent venue for posting product reviews. One of the best ways to bring awareness to a product is to write a review and post it to your blog. Let's say you have a golf blog with a readership of amateur golfers. What a great place to introduce products that those readers would be interested in. If there is a particular kind of golf ball or clothing they enjoy using, you can write a review, post it to your blog, and embed your affiliate link.

Follow High-Profile Blogs

On the flip side of blog marketing is following the blogs of high-profile experts in your industry or who have a market similar to yours. Subscribe to their blogs and pay attention to what they write. You can add relevant comments to the posts to help establish yourself as an expert, too.

Be sure your comments are substantive. Let's say you are a disaster-relief expert, and a leading expert in this industry blogs about steps communities can take during a disaster. Your comment might be:

Excellent points on dealing with a natural disaster. Something I have found to be extremely important is to put systems in place for the protection of pets. This is an often overlooked need during a disaster, but one that pet owners really want to know about. Here are a few simple steps to protect your animals:

➥ Post a sticker on a front and rear window indicating how many animals are in your home.

➥ Keep your dogs' leashes close by in case of an emergency.

➥ Put your cats' carrying cases within close reach for fast evacuation.

These three simple steps can make all the difference in the world.

Some extremely high-profile blogs do not allow comments.

Be Respectful

When you post comments on someone else's *open-comment* blog, be careful not to overtly promote yourself or your business, or your comments might be deleted. If comments go through an approval process, it is likely yours won't be approved if you are blatantly promoting something. The more respectful and valuable your comments, the more likely they will be approved. The more comments you have approved, the more visibility you receive. The more visibility you receive, the more traffic to your own blog or website.

You as a Guest Blogger

A great way to build your visibility and credibility is as a guest blogger. It's not hard at all to find opportunities to be a guest blogger, especially if you are well-known in your industry. Often it is a welcome relief to a blog owner to host a guest blogger; it relieves some of the pressure of constantly creating fresh material.

The more you post on your own blog, the easier the opportunity becomes. If you write consistently, you're a good writer, and your readers are engaged, that's what most blog owners are interested in with their guest bloggers.

Simply ask the blog owner if they would like some fresh content. Not all blog owners will welcome your offer, but many will. Recently my project manager searched out blogs where I could provide a guest post. I was conducting a promotion that added affiliate links to their blogsites for a product I was releasing. Any sales they got through their link generated a 50 percent commission. It was a win/win – they got content from an expert, I got new eyeballs on my information, and we generated sales that benefitted the blog owners, me, and the new customers. Within a very short period of time we secured more than twenty opportunities, and the blog owners welcomed the offer.

It's important to let the blog owner know what you want to write about and to find out if they have a preference about what you write. Determine when your content needs to be delivered and be sure to deliver it on time. It would be a shame to set up a guest-blogging opportunity and not deliver when expected.

Don't be too self-serving when approaching blog owners for a guest spot. Just today I received an email from a complete stranger asking if they could write a blog post for me. I asked if they planned to promote anything and they sent me a link to a website that was very promotional, selling low-end business services. In all good conscience I wasn't able to allow that post. Without knowing the person or the services they were promoting, it would not have been a wise choice to allow a post from this person.

Guest blogging can help you gain high visibility in your market. Once you have name recognition, the rules of the game change.

Increase SEO

Search engine optimization (SEO) is one reason to add fresh content to your blog on a regular basis. Google and other search engines can give you better ranking when they have new keywords to work with. Of course it also ensures fresh reading for your subscribers and those who are searching out blogs in your niche.

Encourage your readers to comment on your posts. This is an often-overlooked aspect of getting reader interaction and more attention for your blog. At the end of a post, simply add "Your comments welcome" or "What is your opinion?" If your topic is controversial, you will likely get quite a few comments. Although you can respond to comments with something as simple as "Thank you for your comment, Bob," a more thoughtful response lets them know you truly appreciate their contribution.

Don't Do All the Heavy Lifting

As previously mentioned, you don't need to create all the content for your blog. You can invite guest bloggers, and you can find other postings that would be of interest to your readers, write a short amount of lead-in information, and add a permalink to the post you are referencing.

Visibility through Creative Blog Marketing

There are lots of numbers floating around the Internet as to how many blogs there actually are. In July of 2008, Technorati claimed to be tracking 112.8 million blogs, a number that likely did not include the over 72 million Chinese blogs as counted by The China Internet Network Information Center at about the same time. In 2011, www.statista.com claimed there were over 186 million blogs worldwide. (Many blog statistics include only the English language blogosphere and not the millions of other blogs around the world.)

So why are these outdated statistics important? These enormous numbers, even though outdated, tell us that you have to do more than just create your blog for it to be an effective tool for marketing, selling, and generating revenue. The idea is to attract a steady stream of visitors who either return to your blog regularly or read your posts via feeds.

As with defining your market, the clearer you are about the purpose of your blog, the better; however, a blog is not meant to be stagnant. It should be a fluid resource that provides opportunities to explore your creativity. One of the benefits of blogging is that you can say and do just about anything you want; and one of the problems of blogging is that you can say and do just about anything you want. ☺

You never know who might find your blog, and that's why it's important to determine what your blog is for, what you want to accomplish, and what image you want to project. Then you'll want to work on driving traffic to your blog. You don't want just any traffic; you want *targeted* traffic. The following sections explain how to get eyeballs on your blog.

Blog Directories

A blog directory is exactly what it sounds like – a directory that lists blogs of every description. Two of the most well-known are Blog Catalog and Technorati. You can submit your blog information to directories yourself or save a lot of time, frustration, and stress by hiring a company or virtual assistant who offers this service.

There are hundreds upon hundreds of directories you can post to. For my blog, *The Marketing Mindset*, I hired a company to submit it to directories. I got registered with more than 100 directories for about $100. This was a good price considering the amount of time it would have taken me to do the work myself. Always think in terms of the return on your investment of time and money. A Google search on "Blog Directory Submission Services" brings up lots of choices. A service that submits manually is a better choice than an automated service.

Each directory has its own guidelines for what to post and how to post it. Follow the submission guidelines as closely as possible. Otherwise your efforts will be in vain.

Titles of Your Posts

The title of your blog post is very important. It's where you want to use your keywords – terms people enter in the search field of an Internet search function and that search engines use to generate those search results. The more you use your keywords in your titles and your posts, the more traffic will be driven to your blog. Think through what keywords your market will be searching on and use those in your titles and posts as often as practical.

Permalinks

As discussed in the chapter about surveys, a permalink also drives traffic to your blog. Bloggers love permalinks because they capture specific references to posts or articles related to what bloggers are writing about. Once your post is up and running, post its URL – the permalink – on Twitter, Facebook, Pinterest, Google+, LinkedIn, and other social networks.

Articles
A great way to drive traffic to your blog is with well-written articles. You can expand a blog post into an article and link it back to your blog in the resource box. Remember to include keywords in the article title and the text, especially in the first two paragraphs.

Social Media
As you build your fan group, followers, friends, subscribers, viewers, and connections, you can let people know about your blog. Don't announce every single post, because people get irritated when they are constantly bombarded with what they may view as insignificant information. Announce your posts manually, such as to your Facebook wall, and be selective. For example, a post announcing several events you are hosting would be of interest to many people.

Leave Comments on Other Blogs
As mentioned before, a great way to gain visibility and expert status is to post comments on other people's blogs. You are often allowed to add a web address or blog address to a comment. Depending on the type of blog, I include my actual web address, www.PowerUpForProfits.com, or my Internet marketing blog, www.themarketingmindset.com. This is great "real estate" that provides excellent visibility. Give thought to where you actually would like viewers to click through to. Not everyone who reads your comment will click your URL, but if your comment is informative, there is a good chance some people will.

Avoid leaving comments that don't add any value or insight to a post such as "Nice post." No one will care about that kind of comment. Add something of value to the conversation. For example, if I read a blog post about marketing a book online, I will add something that was not in the original post that would benefit readers.

You can get hundreds of unique visitors to your sites simply by commenting on blogs with high traffic. But if your comments are not of value, it can minimize your credibility.

Tweet Your Permalink

Your permalink should not be the only thing you tweet; vary your tweets with other messages so your followers will be receptive to your permalink tweets. Make it easy for people to re-tweet your post by providing a re-tweet button.

Promote via Hyperlinks in Ebooks and E-reports

Whether you sell or give away your ebook or e-report, you can add your blog link to the document if your blog ties in to the product you are promoting through your ebook or e-report.

Email Your Subscriber List

Though you should not email your subscriber list about each and every blog post, selected announcements can be well received. It's all about WIFM for your reader, listener, or viewer – *What's In It For Me?*

Use a URL Shortener for Your Permalink

Some URLs are long, and your permalink may be clumsy-looking. A number of services like www.tinyurl.com can provide a shorter version of your URL. In some cases shortening the permalink is absolutely necessary. For example, on Twitter you are limited to 140 characters per tweet, and you don't want to waste characters on a long URL.

Blog Tours

Are you looking for a great way to promote your newest book, one that has been on the market for a while, a new product line, or a live event? Do you want more visibility as an author and/ or expert? Blog tours are an excellent venue for this and more.

Blog tours became popular as authors sought a more cost-effective way than book tours to get the word out about their books. In addition to being expensive, for many authors book tours are also extremely ineffective.

Enter the blog tour. It's a virtual tour during which you stop at a number of blogs and post relevant information. The best part is you do it from the comfort of your home, office, or anywhere in the world where you have an Internet connection, eliminating the need to make personal appearances. It's done over a specific period of time, and blog owners each host one stop on your tour (unless, of course, an owner has several blogs included on the tour).

On your tour you can include reviews, interviews, excerpts, short articles, or book trailers – to name just a few – to promote your book or new product. Conducting a tour takes great time management and organizational skills, so you might want to hire an expert to assist you. There are lots of qualified virtual assistants who organize tours.

To add blogs to your tour, do a search on the type of blogs you would like to guest blog on and approach the blog owners with your tour idea. It's important to explain why it would be to their benefit to have you post on their blog.

My Blog Tour

A couple of years ago I conducted a blog tour that included about twenty blog stops. I definitely noticed an increase in traffic to my own website and my blog, as well as increased SEO. One of the nicest benefits was when a blog owner helped promote my "appearance." Another was interacting with readers who left comments. I kept an eye on comments made through-out the day, and when a comment was posted I returned to the blog and commented on the comment.

That kept the energy flowing and made for a great tour stop.

How Much Work Does It Take?

The amount of work for a high-traffic blog and a low-traffic blog is exactly the same. Your goal should be to find blogs with high visibility.

Find the blogs, gain permission from the owner to guest blog, write your post, and help promote your appearance. Although this does take time, when done correctly the benefits are plentiful.

Lots of people are needlessly intimidated by the thought of a blog tour. Heck, if you've written articles, you can do this. Write great content, and you're on your way. The major difference is that you again must gain permission from the owner of the blog. Be sure the blog owner will let you add your short bio with a link to your blog or website. Never write anonymously. After all, the point is visibility, not just to be writing.

Rarely does a guest blogger get paid for postings. Again, you are seeking the benefit of visibility, as well as increased credibility and SEO.

One of the nicest benefits of blog tours is that you can post the same information on several blogs. This is not necessarily advisable, but you can do it. However, there may be times you will be asked to write exclusive content. What this means is you are placing it on only one blog. You have to determine if it is worth the time to create original content. Although this may seem like a lot of work if there's no pay involved, it's a very, very effective way to get visibility. As with anything, the more you use this promotion strategy, the easier it becomes.

Finding Blogs

Before you begin, put a plan together. The plan should include the date of your tour, the types of blogs you want to post to, who your market is, how many blogs you would ideally like to write for, and what you are planning on promoting, if anything. Tours go hand in hand with promoting something new – a book, an event, a product, etc.

You can find tour blogs by simply announcing your desire to guest blog to your social network connections. You can also send a message to your current opt-in subscribers. Avoid accepting every opportunity that comes along or you may be very busy with very little return on your time invested.

Quality Blogs

Check out the blog before contacting the owner to be sure it's of good quality, professional, and active. It takes as much work to post on a so-so blog as it does to post on a highly visited blog, so make the most of your effort.

Look for a Cross-Section of Blogs

Although you want to write for blogs with a market that would be interested in your information, look for various types of blogs in order to reach a cross-section of readers. Contact people in your circle of influence to inquire about guest blogging. If you have a good reputation, it should be relatively easy to find opportunities through them. Check blog directories, blogs listed in the *blogroll* of a popular blog you are targeting, and use Google searches. (A blogroll is a list posted at a blog site of links to other blogs the blogger likes.)

➥ Here are some of the most popular directories:

➥ Technorati http://technorati.com/

➥ Blog Catalog http://www.blogcatalog.com/

➥ On Top List http://www.ontoplist.com/

Contact Blog Owners

To get the greatest result for your efforts, be prepared when approaching blog owners. Let the owner know who you are, what you want, why you would be a nice addition to the blog, what your expertise is, and what the benefit to their readers will be. Avoid being pushy, arrogant, or coming across as a know-it-all. Nothing turns a blog owner off faster than someone acting as if they can "rescue" them in some way.

In some cases you will find a contact form or request form on the site that you need to complete. Otherwise simply send an email. You can also reach many blog owners by direct message via Facebook, Twitter, LinkedIn, and other social networks to which they belong.

Low Risk to the Owner

Do what you can to minimize the risk to the blog owner. After all, if you do poorly with your posting, it reflects on the blog owner. If you do a stellar job, you will likely be invited back. One way to reduce the risk is to have established a track record by posting frequently to your own blog. When you approach the blog owner, you can send samples of your writing by sending permalinks to various postings the owner can review.

Celebrity Status Helps

The more well-known you are, the easier it is to find opportunities, because the blog owner knows you will bring readers with you, help promote your appearance, and increase credibility for the blog owner. It's simply a fact of life. By well-known I mean well-known in your industry, not like Oprah.

Be Active

A way to get noticed by the blog owner is to leave comments on blogs other than your own. For example, if you are a nutritionist, find blogs that those interested in nutrition read. When you read a post on that blog worth commenting on, do so. The more valuable your comments, the more likely you are to get noticed by your potential customers.

Below is a substantial comment I posted some time ago.

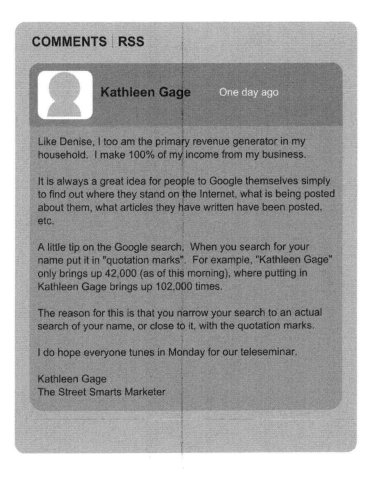

COMMENTS | RSS

Kathleen Gage   One day ago

Like Denise, I too am the primary revenue generator in my household. I make 100% of my income from my business.

It is always a great idea for people to Google themselves simply to find out where they stand on the Internet, what is being posted about them, what articles they have written have been posted, etc.

A little tip on the Google search. When you search for your name put it in "quotation marks". For example, "Kathleen Gage" only brings up 42,000 (as of this morning), where putting in Kathleen Gage brings up 102,000 times.

The reason for this is that you narrow your search to an actual search of your name, or close to it, with the quotation marks.

I do hope everyone tunes in Monday for our teleseminar.

Kathleen Gage
The Street Smarts Marketer

The First Time Is the Most Difficult

Your first blog tour is going to be the most difficult to organize. You might have to approach several blog owners before one says yes. But hang in there; it will be worth it.

A Big No-No!

Avoid sending your completed post before determining the level of interest from the blog owner. You might put a lot of work into writing something only to have it rejected due to word count, inappropriate topic for their readers, and/or the blog owner is just not interested in guest bloggers. And by submitting only the concept or title rather than the complete post, you still have the opportunity to fully customize it to the particular blog audience.

Ask the Right Questions

When a blog owner agrees to either a blog-tour stop or guest blogging, get the answers to these questions:

➥ What is my responsibility? Find out what the owner expects from you. The more you know, the easier the process.

➥ When do they need the post?

➥ How many words would they like?

➥ Who retains copyright? (you should)

➥ What can the blog owner do with your content beyond the guest post?

➥ Can I add images? Will the owner add some?

➥ Do I get access to post directly to the site or do I send the post to the blog owner for publication?

➥ Can I put links in my post?

➥ Does the blog owner want to be an affiliate and post their affiliate link at the end of my post?

Create Your Post

Write your post based on the format, word count, etc., provided by the blog owner. Keep their audience in mind and deliver everything as agreed upon and before the deadline. Find out if they want exclusive content or a post that you will submit to several blogs. Always do a *stellar* job. There is no point going through all the effort required to get this opportunity and not putting your best foot forward.

Help Promote Your Post

You will make blog owners very happy when you drive traffic to their blog. You can tweet about it, write about it, submit media releases, announce it on your Facebook wall, post it as an event in online calendars, etc. Set up a page with articles, tips, tweets, excerpts (if you are promoting a book), and anything else that makes the job of the blog owner as easy as possible. The more you do, the more visibility everyone gets, and the more likely you will be asked back.

Respond to Comments

Keep an eye on the comments made about your post. The more interactive you are, the better. Post reminders to your daily schedule to check for, and respond to, comments. Most blog platforms will alert you when a comment is made, and that's the best way to track them, so sign up for that service.

In Conclusion

Blog tours and guest blogging are great ways to market. It's a little-used strategy, and one you would be wise to incorporate into your marketing mix sooner rather than later.

Chapter 9

Instant Credibility through Article Marketing

Article Marketing

Although not everyone needs name recognition within their market, 99 percent of the clients I work with find that name recognition is essential to their success. If you are an author, coach, speaker, trainer, consultant, artist, or entrepreneur, you likely need name recognition.

One of the most effective ways to get your name recognized is by writing and distributing articles – article marketing. I began article marketing in the late nineties when few people were doing it. I had very little visibility and market position compared to what I have today. Without a doubt, one thing that skyrocketed my visibility was article marketing.

If you haven't yet begun writing articles to establish your expert status, build your subscriber list, and increase your credibility and market reach, now is a great time to begin. Article marketing:

➤➤ Positions you as an expert

➤➤ Increases traffic to your blog, website, and landing pages

➤➤ Increases sales potential

➤➤ Builds name recognition

➤➤ Gains trust and entry into your customer's mind

➤➤ Builds a highly responsive subscriber list for any industry

Not Everyone Agrees

Years ago I received a very heated email from a subscriber who said article marketing for visibility, credibility, and increased revenues absolutely *does not* work. She claimed she tried this strategy with no success at all, and she was very upset. She supported her position by adding that many of her friends and colleagues had similar results. Here's what she wrote: "I personally don't know anyone who has gotten increased business from this tactic and none of my clients have either. Who is getting more business from this and what are they doing differently?"

Amazingly, the very strategy she said didn't work was what

had encouraged her to opt in to my subscriber list – she read one of my articles and responded to the free ebook offer mentioned at the end of the article. Hmmmm.

Success Strategies

It takes more than just throwing some words together and calling it an article for article marketing to work. Consider the following questions:

» How well written is the article?

» Is it geared to a specific market?

» Does the title grab people's attention?

» Is there a resource box at the end of the article?

» Does the resource box include a compelling offer that encourages the reader to visit your website, blog, or landing page?

» Is your website set up to optimize those visits with a visible opt-in opportunity that is of high value?

» Do you have a follow-up plan to market to those who opt in to your subscriber list?

» Are you creating high value for those who receive messages from you?

When one or more of these elements is not in place, writing and distributing articles can be completely ineffective.

Be Realistic

Don't expect to immediately increase revenue by posting one article. There's a process involved in turning casual readers into paying customers, and this process should be part of your overall marketing strategy. It's like baking a cake; if you don't have all the right ingredients and use them in the correct order, you can have a total flop on your hands. But when article marketing is coordinated with the rest of your marketing plan, you can be extremely successful and enjoy a very tasty outcome.

There's Always the Need

There's a constant need for fresh content from online article directories, trade journal publishers, magazines, websites, blogs, and ezine publishers, to name just a few. Although there are countless people submitting articles online every single day, the majority try this strategy for a while and then move on to something else. Those of us who realize the long-term benefits make sure to distribute articles on a regular basis. It is not unusual for an article to get a response weeks, months, and even years after it has been posted.

This timeless content is called *evergreen.* If your main distribution strategy is directories, evergreen is essential. Article marketing via blog posts can be more time sensitive.

Top Three Mistakes

The top three reasons why article marketing sometimes doesn't work are lack of focus on the market, poorly written content, and a weak title. Other reasons include minimal distribution, less-than-optimal word count, and not including a call to action in your article.

Know Your Market

As with the other marketing strategies discussed above, be sure to know who your market is, what type of information they seek, and what you can write about that will generate interest and a provide solution for them.

➨ Who are you writing for?

➨ What do they want to know?

➨ Why do they want to know this?

➨ How will you help them solve their problem?

➨ How is your information different from that of others who claim to be experts on the topic?

With the answers to these questions, you will be in a better position to effectively reach your readers.

148

Where to Find Out What They Want

If you don't know what your readers are interested in, ask them. Surveys are very powerful and underutilized tools for everything from article writing, report development, and media release content to full-blown product development. Don't assume you can create information without having a clear understanding of what your market wants, needs, and is willing to pay for. Refer back to Chapter 5 – "Do You Know What They Want?" – about how to conduct a survey.

You can also get tons of fresh ideas for topics by visiting article directories and reading articles by other experts on your topic or industry. Notice what topics are commented on in blogs, forums, and social networks. Pay close attention to what your customers are frustrated about. What keeps them awake at night? What conversations are you having with them?

Here is a very simple formula for article development:

Step One – Decide on topics based on your market and your expertise.

Step Two – Create a list of six to twelve titles. They should be short and catchy – seven words or less in most cases. (There are always exceptions to any rule.)

Step Three – Set a target date to complete your articles.

Step Four – Write at least six quality articles. Word count can be from 250 to 750. A high word count is not necessarily the best choice; quality content is more important. Be sure to optimize your articles with keywords.

Step Five – Get your articles copyedited if necessary.

Step Six – Add a well-crafted resource box with a permalink driving visitors to your blog, website, or landing page. A *permalink*, also referred to as an *anchor link*, is a link that when clicked takes someone directly to a specific blog post. A *landing page*, also referred to as a *squeeze page* and an *opt-in page*, is used to build your list.

Step Seven – Develop a list of locations to submit your articles to. To jumpstart your online presence, submit at least three articles a week for a six-week period. There are plenty of article directories online to choose from. A quick Google search with the words "article directories" will bring up plenty of choices.

Step Eight – Distribute your articles.

Step Nine – Repeat.

Article Development and Distribution Process

Ghostwriters and Private Label Rights (PLR)

If the thought of writing your own articles is less appealing than having a root canal, there are solutions. You can hire a ghostwriter, or you can use what is called private label rights (PLR).

A ghostwriter is someone you hire to write for you and you take the piece on as your own. *Private label rights* is a concept used in Internet marketing and derived from private labeling. It's a license whereby the author sells most or all of the intellectual property rights to their work. The license is defined by the author of the work and has no legal definition.

While licenses differ with each author and seller, the basic idea is that the license permits buyers to rebrand the content under their own name and brand (excluding copyright). This means that the product can be modified, sold, resold, or repurposed in many different formats.

The one downside of PLR is that many article directories do *not* let you post anything with PLR, so be sure to check the rules and regulations of directories.

Word Count

Keep your articles short and to the point. An average article has 400 to 750 words. Shorter can actually be better since readers often experience information overload. Don't add to this common problem. If you can say in 250 words what others are saying in 700, your articles will likely be considered extremely valuable. Check each directory for the minimum word count of an article. It varies from directory to directory.

Titles

A title can make or break a piece. Although you may be tempted to use "cutesy" titles, keep in mind that you are also using the title and copy for search engine optimization. Make it catchy *and* include keywords. Avoid ambiguous titles that do not convey to the reader what the article is about.

SEO

It's important to include targeted keywords in the title and throughout the body of your article. When I was doing a lot of promotions for my training program called "How to Become an Amazon.com Bestseller,"I made sure to include keywords in the titles and bodies of my articles, and it made a huge difference. I got very high rankings in searches with this focused approach.

Let's say you are a hiking expert and hiking is the main subject you write about. Use *Hiking* in the title, such as, "Ten Keys to Superb Hiking Locations" or "Hiking – Ten Top Locations throughout the World." These titles allow both visitors and search engines to know what your article is about. When you can't tell what an article is about, you don't read further, do you?

Description for Directories

Some directories ask for a short description of your article, so prepare your description before contacting directories for article placement. Be sure to use keywords in your description as well. An example for the hiking article would be:

Finding the perfect hiking locations can be tough. In "Ten Keys to Superb Hiking Locations," readers learn where the best hiking locations are.

Where to Post Your Articles

There are an unlimited number of locations where you can post your articles. Directories, forums, social networks, and blogs are the most common. Depending on your market, you might want to post your articles on your trade association's website, the electronic version of a trade journal, or a private membership site. The possibilities are endless.

When you find a good location, contact the decision maker to find out if they are interested. In some cases they want original content that will be available only on their site. Your goals, how valuable the location is, and what the long-term benefits are determine whether this is a good choice. I usually avoid exclusive-rights locations because of their limited reach. But if it allows me to reach a very exclusive part of my market or increases my status as an expert, I consider it. As before, always keep in mind *return on investment.*

No Skill, No Desire, No Time

Perhaps you want to get articles to market, but for any number of reasons you are unable to write them. Not to worry; there are solutions. The first very viable option is to hire a ghostwriter. There are plenty of writers looking for work. Here are a few places to find them:

➻ Your immediate circle of influence
➻ Social networks you belong to
➻ Forums you belong to
➻ Directories for contractors such as www.elance.com and www.odesk.com
➻ Craigslist

When hiring a ghostwriter, determine the turnaround time, costs, what they specialize in (if anything), and whether they have samples of their work and references you can contact. Avoid unpleasant misunderstandings by getting as much information up front as possible.

Getting Over Writer's Block

Writer's block can prevent you from not only writing articles, but moving into information product development as well. Here are proven strategies to help you overcome writer's block:

➻ Set aside time to write. Some people say they have to be inspired, but if you wait until you are inspired, you may never get over writer's block.
➻ Start with something short. You don't have to write the next great novel in one sitting. Writing is a process.
➻ Take a walk to clear your head. It's easy to get stuck when you don't take periodic breaks. A short walk can help a lot.
➻ Set a deadline.

➼ Do some free-form writing, which is writing whatever comes to mind. Once you get some words on paper, it can be easier to organize your thoughts.

➼ Outline your article; it makes the task much less overwhelming. Many excellent writers outline everything they write beforehand.

Article Visibility

Writing your article is one thing; gaining visibility is the next important step. Do all you can to gain as much visibility as possible for your articles. You put a lot of effort into writing them, so be proactive in getting them in front of as many readers as possible.

Directories

An *article directory* is a website with a collection of articles about various subjects. Not all directories are worth submitting your articles to. You are better off submitting your work to six to twelve high-quality directories than to hundreds of mediocre ones. There are free directories that will not pay you for your articles, but there are lots of directories that will pay you to participate.

A *resource box,* also known as an *author box,* can be provided for personal information about you, including a link to your website. *Tags,* or *categories,* are often used by directories to organize articles and help with searches. They act as keywords to identify topics covered in the articles.

In some cases your articles become available as soon as you submit them, and some directories review articles before publishing and it takes several days for them to appear. This helps to eliminate low-quality submissions, including duplicate articles, spam, and spun articles.

Be sure your market visits the directories you choose. It is better to use fewer targeted directories than dozens that have little, if any traffic.

Blog

Post your articles to your blog. This is just the first step of using your blog for article marketing. Tweet something about the article with your permalink in the tweet. Post something similar to your tweet on your Facebook wall. Be sure to include the permalink. Post the permalink at other social network locations such as LinkedIn.

Twitter

Post a short bit about your article (a good descriptive title is often enough) at Twitter using your blog posting permalink or your directory permalinks. Announce your article on Twitter several times the day you post it, since your followers don't always see all of your postings.

Facebook

Post a short bit about your article on your Facebook wall and include the permalinks from both your blog and directories.

Integrate

Set up your blog, Facebook account, and other social networks so that your tweets are displayed in specific areas. If you are not familiar with how to do this you can find plenty of people at www.odesk.com who are available for hire.

Guest Blogging

Plenty of blog owners are looking for great content. If your articles are well done, there is a good chance you can find plenty of opportunities to be a guest blogger.

Blog Carnivals

(The following description comes directly from the FAQ section of Blog Carnival Magazine.) A blog carnival is a particular kind of blog community. There are many kinds of blogs with articles on many kinds of topics. Blog carnivals typically collect links pointing to blog articles on a particular topic. It's like a magazine, with a title, topic, editors, contributors, an audience, and editions that typically come out on a regular basis such as every Monday, or on the first of the month. Each edition is a special blog article that consists of links to all the contributions that have been submitted, often with the editor's opinions or remarks.

Autoresponder

You can add a series of articles to an *autoresponder* – a program that responds to emails automatically – specific to something your subscribers download, for example a four- to seven-day on-line training course.

Website

Put a page up on your website with links to your articles.

Encourage Others

Invite others to use your articles as long as they give you full credit. Article marketing is one of the best ways to drive extremely targeted traffic to any website. Just be sure to develop a systemized approach so it's as effective as possible.

When you are strategic about getting your articles posted in various locations you can gain lots of visibility. The more you have in print, both online and off, the more of an expert you are viewed as.

Chapter 10

The Greatest Thing since Sliced Bread – Social Media

One of the greatest changes to happen online is social networks and social media. Social media has changed the way people communicate with each other online and offers a greater opportunity than ever to share your message with the world. It offers incredible opportunities for entrepreneurs and small business owners looking for their own perfect clients. It has leveled the playing field for virtually any entrepreneur in any industry.

Using social media makes it possible to connect, communicate, and create relationships with people all over the globe who are in need of your product. You establish these relationships by creating compelling profiles about you and your business and compelling free content so those perfect clients can get to know you and learn what you stand for and how they can work with you.

Social Networks

A *social network* is an online community of people with similar interests. It's a social structure made of up individuals and organizations called *nodes* that are connected by one or more specific commonalities such as friendship, family, industries, knowledge bases, religions, etc.

There are very specific social networks and very broad-based social networks. Most are web-based and offer emailing options, postings for anyone in your immediate network to see, and instant messaging or direct messaging.

A word of caution: Not everyone is who they appear to be at social networks, so be advised not to give out too much personal information. For example, if you post your birthday, don't include the year of your birth for all to see. This is one small measure you can take to prevent identity theft. And don't post that you will be away from home. There are people looking for this kind of information. What better target for home burglary than someone who tells the world they will be away for a while?

There are new social networks cropping up all the time. At the time of this writing these were some of the most popular for the general populace:

- Facebook
- Twitter
- LinkedIn
- Pinterest
- Google+
- YouTube

The beauty of most social media is that you can announce new information products, events, partnerships, and other such things to drive traffic to your blog, website, and/or landing pages, thus building your credibility, opt-in subscriber list, and market interest.

In some social media networks you can set up private groups. I have several private groups for various reasons. For my high-end clients I have a private Facebook group that only they have access to. In it I post information that the general public is not privy to. This is a very effective way to create added value for specific groups of people. I am a member of several private groups, too – everything from book groups to online marketers and social entrepreneurs.

What Exactly Is Social Media?

There are countless definitions of *social media*, and many are so ambiguous and confusing that they can leave someone more in the dark than before they heard or read the definition. *Social media* is a creative term used to describe tools such as blogs, podcasts, wikis, and social networking sites where people create content, share it with each other, and connect. It's simply a way to keep in touch with people online using social networks.

Social media is also an umbrella term that defines the various activities that integrate technology, social interaction, words, and pictures shared online. It's based on user-developed content found on social networks such as Facebook, Twitter, LinkedIn, Pinterest, Google+, and YouTube focused on user interaction and involvement. Understanding social media and social media marketing (SMM) is actually very simple, yet many people become overwhelmed due to the complexity of some of the social network sites.

User-Created Content

Social media content is user-created video, audio, text, and multimedia published and shared in a social environment such as a blog, social network, forum, or video. You use hosting sites like YouTube, Flickr, Facebook, LinkedIn, Squidoo, and other such locations to share your information.

In today's world, *social media marketing* (SMM) is a must-do for virtually any business, large or small, that is serious about building an online presence, so don't resist learning about this most important marketing tool. Think of it this way: When the telephone was first introduced to the general public there were actually quite a few people who said they just didn't need that "crazy device"; there are many people who feel the same way about SMM, but if you are not yet participating in the top sites, you can fall behind very quickly.

Social media marketing is the online version of public relations, customer service, loyalty building, collaboration, networking, and thought leadership. Not only can you market yourself and your business through social media for very little financial investment, but you can keep in touch with a global market, connect with people you did not have access to in the past, and gain market reach very, very quickly.

One of the greatest benefits of social media marketing is the opportunity to position yourself as a thought leader. Without it there were incredible restrictions to getting your voice out to the market. Today there are few, if any restrictions. You can easily position your voice, beliefs, and philosophy through any number of channels available on the Internet.

One of my favorite shows is *The Voice*. In each season of *The Voice*, at least one contestant is discovered through their online presence. Many who in the past could not get their voice heard now have a platform through their blog. YouTube is a great platform for building a strong following. A few years ago, Gary Vaynerchuk was a complete unknown online; today he is a recognized YouTube personality and a wine industry expert. He started out by posting a few videos online. From there he grew into a recognized personality by regularly posting short videos on YouTube. You can do the same. All you need is a voice and the willingness to get your voice out to market. The more unique your voice and the more you can be yourself, the more success you will likely have. Avoid trying to be like others. There are already plenty of clones online. To be your unique self you need a message, a point, and insights that are of value to others.

Position your message by consistently posting to various locations. The more consistent you are, the better. In social media marketing, one plus one equals hundreds and even thousands. Traditional marketing is a one-way conversation; not so with SMM. It's about having a dialogue rather than a monologue. This is the greatest change we have seen in marketing in decades.

You Need a Presence

According to a recent study by Cone Business in Social Media, "93% of Americans believe that a company should have a presence on social media sites and 85% believe that these companies should use these services to interact with consumers." Here are some other interesting data points from the study:

➡ 60% of Americans regularly interact with companies on a social media site

➡ 43% of consumers say that companies should use social networks to solve the consumers' problems

➤ 41% believe that companies should use social media tools to solicit feedback on products and services

➤ Men are more likely to use social media tools to interact with a company than women (33% vs. 17%)

➤ 33% of younger consumers (18-34) and those with household incomes over $75,000 believe that companies should try to market to them through social networks

The Internet has opened up worldwide communications with very few boundaries. If you are not yet convinced, then you are going to be left behind.

Before jumping into the SMM game, determine your purpose for being involved. For most small businesses the reasons are likely one or more of the following:

➤ Gain global visibility

➤ Stay in touch with existing customers

➤ Secure leads for potential customers

➤ Network

➤ Establish market position and brand recognition

➤ Join groups with like-minded people

➤ Build community

➤ Establish expert status

➤ Collaborate with other experts

A Huge Challenge

The greatest challenge of SMM is knowing which locations are most beneficial to your goals. It's very easy to get distracted by "bright, shining objects." Gaining the most benefit for the time you invest with social media takes focus, discipline, and commitment. It doesn't happen by chance, but rather by design.

Find the locations and spend time where colleagues, potential and current customers, and others that are a fit for your market hang out. This means you need to research social media locations before jumping in.

Be a Resource

Think in terms of how you can contribute and establish yourself as a reliable resource. Although social media definitely includes marketing and sales of products, it is essential not to view your involvement solely in terms of making sales. This is the old model of marketing. If all you do is sell, sell, sell, people will ignore you in fast order. Think in terms of networking, building relationships, and holding conversations. Social media and social networking are simply global approaches to connecting with people. Be a resource rather than a vendor. Have a unique message.

Lots of People Are Wrong

When I first began my involvement with social media, I made the same mistake many people do – I went for quantity rather than quality. Today I do the opposite. I would much rather have a small network of friends, followers, and subscribers who are interactive and responsive to my information than thousands upon thousands of connections who could care less about what I have to say. And I can't possibly pay attention to what thousands and thousands of people have to say to me.

A Global Reach Is Very Attainable

Social media marketing allows you to have a global reach with a minimum of investment. Solopreneurs used to have very limited market reach. Of course you can invest substantial money, but you don't need a lot of money to get started. There is an investment of time, but when you consider the return on that investment, it becomes a nonissue.

Where Are Your Competitors?

It's likely your competitors are already in the social media arena. If they are and you aren't, ouch! You are setting yourself up for defeat. Don't get left behind. Even if you don't think you need to be using SMM, your customers likely think you should.

With more and more people jumping on the bandwagon every day, your customers probably have, too.

Common Concerns

Even though SMM is very important, some people worry about finding time, negative feedback, and where to participate.

Time

Finding time can be a great challenge. This is why I recommend you plan and schedule your social media marketing time. Don't go from zero to sixty in one fell swoop. Start slowly. Observe for a while and then get involved. Schedule time for posting, commenting, and responding. Start with a short period of time first thing in the morning and then again later in the day. Many people use timers to assure they won't spend too much time at the various networks they belong to.

Negative Feedback

The more visible you are, the more of a target you become. If you can't deal with something negative being posted about you, it's likely you are not going to make it online.

If something negative is posted about you, don't react right away. Read what has been posted, take a break from it, and go back and read it again. The question to ask is, "Is there validity to what is being said or is it simply malicious?"

If you have a stellar reputation and something negative is posted, often your supporters will come to your aid and post rebuttals. However, if the information posted is truly malicious, slanderous, and downright false, plan your response carefully. Stick to facts, don't respond in anger, and, most important, be honest, transparent, and level-headed.

Where to Participate

Before immediately jumping into a particular social network, do a bit of research. It's a pretty safe bet that locations such as Facebook, Twitter, and LinkedIn are great places for you to be, but investigate the activities of social networks you're considering. If your market is extremely niched, the most popular locations might not be the best use of your time. Let's say you are a dental professional wanting to reach other dental professionals. A location like Web Dental would be a better use of your time than Facebook for this particular market. But if you're a dentist wanting to reach potential patients, you could use Facebook very effectively by localizing your efforts.

In traditional marketing, much was measured by return on investment (ROI): If you spend X you should get Y in return. Not so with social media. Blogs, Facebook, Twitter, and other social media were never intended for push-marketing messages. They are intended to be personal communication tools. However, now that some social networks offer advertising, there is a focus on ROI for some investments.

In most cases basing your involvement on direct returns for time and money invested is not the best measurement; it is the amount of interaction you receive – how many blog comments, re-tweets, wall comments, and comments on videos. However, there are ways you can get immediate returns on your time invested. A great example is Facebook events postings where you can see real-time results in the form of confirms, maybes, and declines.

Plan, Schedule, and Participate

Develop a plan for what you want to accomplish through SMM. If you plan to use various locations to establish name recognition and visibility, determine where you are going to get the greatest result for your involvement.

It is not uncommon for people to start off with a bang and

then little by little put their social media marketing on the back burner. For example, you might begin posting daily or even two or three times a day to your blog, then cut back to three times a week. Then once a week. Then every couple of weeks. Then.... . Sticking to a posting schedule, even if that means starting out with once per week, reflects more positively on you and gains you more credibility. It's the same with social networks, forums, and other locations.

Here's a shortcut for getting maximum exposure with an investment of as little as twenty minutes a day: Start by answering the question, "What would my community be most interested in? What's a problem they need a solution to?" Based on the answers, focus your efforts on:

➤ The topic
➤ The best locations
➤ The efficiency of what you're doing

Create a short video or audio file and post it at locations your market frequents (you can repurpose it down the road). Offer only information that is of interest to your market.

Create your video using Camtasia or MacTalk, and audio using Dragon or Windows' speech recognition software. All you need is an inexpensive microphone to do this. When you have recorded a few minutes of content, read it and clean it up; there are likely to be glaring mistakes in the content you recorded. Once you clean it up, you can use as is or re-record it with anything you added in for a clean recording in audio or video format. This is a quick way to write your script for your presentation. Next:

➤ Turn the script into articles, and the articles into blog posts.
➤ Post a short description with the permalink at Facebook and LinkedIn.
➤ Take snippets out of the articles and blog posts to create tweets.
➤ Put the main points on slides and upload them to SlideShare.

➤ Record a short presentation and create a video to go on You-Tube.

➤ Post the audio file as a podcast at iTunes.

If you don't want to do all the detail work, send your recording to a virtual assistant (VA) for transcription and then complete the other steps above. This should take no longer than twenty to thirty minutes. The amount of reach and SEO you will get is beyond anything else you can do in twenty or thirty minutes. But as always, be sure you know who your market is and what keywords they will be searching on, otherwise your information will go out to the wrong people and your efforts will be for naught. Try this for thirty days and see what happens to your rankings.

Schedule

The majority of successful participants in social media schedule time for what they know must be done, whether it be interacting in social networks and forums, posting articles or media releases, posting videos, or posting blog comments. You will get a lot more accomplished if you schedule specific activities on your calendar.

Some time ago I signed up for a thirty-day blogging course. It was in the form of an ebook with the recommendation to do one lesson per day for thirty days. To get the most from my investment, I scheduled a one-hour block of time each day for thirty days to optimize my study time. If I got the lesson done in a shorter period of time, I used the extra time for review or to implement a lesson. Had I not scheduled the time and committed to following the schedule, I likely would not have completed the training. I would have started out with the best of intentions, but I would have gotten sidetracked in no time at all.

Making time to do something and sticking with it is a challenge for most of us, and it's the same with social media.

Participate

Success depends on your participation in the various social networks you join. If you simply register and hide behind an invisible curtain, you are doing no good for yourself or others. You must participate.

Remember, this is about getting your voice heard. You have something to say; you stand for something; you want to see a change; you are a social entrepreneur – don't lose sight of this. Get involved and give something back if you want to get something out of your time invested.

Make it easy for people to interact with you, keeping in mind that not everyone is who they say they are. As you become more visible online, there will be times when your whereabouts are posted by others. For example, when I attend or speak at conferences it is not uncommon for others to post something like "Got to meet Kathleen Gage at XYZ conference," so I have learned to take safety precautions by posting something about my house sitter being at my home during my absence. This isn't necessary in every situation, but the more public you become, the more you need to consider such precautions.

But *do* become a "real" person online. Get to know others and let them get to know you as a person rather than as your brand. As you reveal things about yourself, your market gravitates to this information. They are attracted by who you are as a person, what you stand for, and what you believe in. I love my animals, animal rescue, time in my garden, time with my family, hiking, diversity, and spiritual studies. I have incorporated stories about these activities on my blog, in my wall postings, and in videos. By doing this I have attracted a tribe of people who enjoy similar things.

During the time my father passed on and my mother was extremely ill, I shared my thoughts and feelings about these experiences. I didn't do so for any reason other than being called to do so. What I didn't realize was how much this would resonate with my market. I became more of a complete person to them. Granted, there were some people who didn't care at all about what I was going through, and many of them opted off my list. This was fine with me.

I long ago realized that I am not for everyone nor is everyone for me. This flies in the face of conventional wisdom. In the past we tried to reach as many people as possible and offer a solution to as many people as possible. Today it's about building communities or, as Seth Godin calls our communities, our tribes. This makes working with one's market very enjoyable. Rather than operating solely from a business perspective, we have a holistic approach to what we do. This approach will serve you, too. Be a complete person to your market. Be who you are, not a fabricated persona that even you can't relate to.

The Long Haul versus the Short Term

If you want to be successful at social media marketing, go for the long haul and avoid the "get in and clean up" attitude. As a socially conscious entrepreneur, it's likely you have a broad perspective, but honestly, we sometimes get caught up in the flavor-of-the-month club – what is being touted as the latest and greatest way to reach one's market and make lots of money.

I am all for making lots of money, but I am more for being in alignment with my message. When I am clear on this and do the necessary and appropriate footwork, the money definitely follows. If you view SMM as a short-term project, there is likely a better way to use your time. Building relationships is not a short-term proposition.

Build It and They Won't Come

The *Field of Dreams* "build it and they will come" mentality is not at all true when it comes to SMM. They have to know it has been built, and telling them is part of the process. This is why you have to be actively involved.

Know When to Quit

Although it's beneficial to be active in various social networks, you also have to know when you are too involved. It is very easy to get sucked into various social networks and spend hour upon hour doing what may seem like productive activities, but before you know it your day is done with little, if anything truly productive completed. This is why scheduling time is important; not only will it keep you involved, it will help you avoid over-involvement.

Don't Jump and then Look

Sometimes we hear about the latest and greatest regarding social media and immediately jump on board. But most innovations are not one-size-fits-all. Do your research. Find out if a particular network is going to help you achieve your goals. There are thousands upon thousands of networks to choose from, and there is no way you can cover all of the various locations.

In Conclusion

As with the many other visibility strategies in *Power Up for Profits,* social media can catapult your visibility and market reach when done right. On the flip side it can be a complete waste of time. Because it is so important to your overall market position, I recommend you reread this chapter several times. Fully understanding the power of social media, being extremely strategic about your involvement and your message, and doing something each and every day can get you amazing results.

Begin today to make this happen.

Chapter 11

Credibility through What Others Say – Testimonials

Credibility through Testimonials

Most everyone is looking for ways to enhance their credibility. One of the most effective ways to enhance your credibility and trust with prospective customers is for other people to sing your praises. The best way to do this? With strong testimonials. When you have great testimonials, virtually all you do is enhanced.

Testimonials are third-party evidence as to the benefit of what you are selling; they work like a reference on your resume. They are much more likely to be believed than ads, direct mail, or your saying how wonderful you are. New customers often make buying decisions based on testimonials.

A testimonial is a written or spoken statement about the experience someone has had with you, your product, or your company. Written testimonials are the norm, but more and more people are posting audio and video testimonials. They can be used on your website or in your marketing material, media kit, brochure, or book.

Because there has been so much hype, scamming, and false information in testimonials, things have changed drastically over the last decade regarding what we can and cannot do, say, and write. There are very strict guidelines set down by the Federal Trade Commission (FTC). Be sure to read the FTC guidelines about testimonials before you secure and post them. You will save yourself a lot of trouble in the long run.

Make Them Real

Authentic positive customer feedback is a powerful marketing tool. Benefits include:

➻ Establishing your credibility quickly

➻ Setting yourself apart from your competition

➻ Quickly and easily demonstrating the benefits of your product or customer service

Potential customers are more likely to believe your trustworthy customers than your tooting your own horn.

Tips for Securing Effective Testimonials

Carefully choose customers who provide testimonials, making sure each one represents the kind of customer you want to work with. Use the ideal client profile from your market analysis.

If you've been in business for any length of time, it is easier to secure testimonials than if you are brand new at what you do. But you can get testimonials even if you're new. A very effective way to secure testimonials is to offer a trial version of your product in exchange for a testimonial. If you're just starting out, this is a great way to secure feedback. For example, if you are marketing a new ebook, offer a review copy to a select number of people whose opinions matter to your market.

Another way is to ask for feedback via email, a web form, or an automated voice mail system from those who purchase your product. When someone sends you an email saying how wonderful you or your product is, ask them if you can use it as a testimonial.

Getting "HOT" testimonials

Ask the following two questions to keep things on track:

- ➤➤ What did the product specifically do to improve the way you do [*whatever it is your product is designed to help the client with*]?
- ➤➤ If someone were to ask you about this product, what would you say?

Unsolicited Comments

If you have stellar products, customers will often email you to tell you how much value they have received. Simply respond with a request to use their statement as a testimonial. Here is one such testimonial I received:

> I just wanted to let you know that the info you are providing is GREAT! When I graduated in 1992 with my marketing degree, Internet Marketing wasn't part of the curriculum. I can't tell you how much fear and anxiety I had associated with social media, blogging and all the rest. And not only that, I was completely overwhelmed with where to start. I can honestly say that after only two lessons, I am feeling so much more comfortable with all of it and loving the process you are taking me through to set the foundation. I am actually looking forward to being able to integrate this into my marketing plan.
>
> ~Theresa~

I immediately emailed Theresa and asked her if I could use her email as a testimonial. She gave full permission. By being proactive with this approach you will have more usable testimonials.

Relevance

Testimonials should reflect the type of customer you want to continue to attract. For example, if you want to attract small business owners, secure testimonials from small business owners rather than corporate CEOs. If you want to expand your corporate client base, testimonials from solopreneurs will not be as effective as those from your corporate target market.

Who Is Most Credible?

Although "celebrity" testimonials can be very nice to add to your marketing material, website, and blog, often testimonials from "regular" folks work even better, because your potential customer has more in common with them than a celebrity, and finds them more believable. On the other hand, a celebrity endorsement carries a lot of weight. Much depends on your market and what it is you are promoting.

Be Sure You Have Permission

To ensure you have no future problems with using testimonials, be sure you have permission to use them. Don't assume that because someone sends you an email telling you how fabulous you or your product is that you can use it in your marketing material.

Obtain a Signed and Dated Written Permission

You would be in a world of hurt if you obtained verbal permission and found out after you invested in printed marketing material that the person changed their mind and didn't want you to use their testimonial. It's relatively easy to make changes online, but if you're using printed marketing material, it's not so easy to make changes.

Years ago my primary market was corporate America. After I facilitated a full-day training session for a very large corporation, the meeting planner raved about it. Not only did she call me to tell me how wonderful the day had been, she also sent me an email. I asked her if I could use her email for future promotions. Without hesitation she said yes, so I posted her comments on my website.

Imagine my surprise when she called me in a panic and said I had to take the testimonial down. Without hesitation I did, but I was still confused as to what went wrong. Apparently giving permission to post her comments breached the confidentiality clause of my contract. I could have avoided this problem if I had requested signed consent. She would likely have realized that what I was asking was a breach of contract and declined before I had posted it, saving us both unnecessary frustration. Although this was an isolated incident, it made me more cautious in the future. It is easier to make a change on your website or blog than in printed material, but any change is a hassle involving time and financial expense.

Permission sent via email can be sufficient, but be sure to print the original testimonial and the email giving you permission to use it, and file them with your important documents.

Audio and Video Testimonials

There are many options for audio and video testimonials. A quick Google search will bring up several choices for technology you can use. Consult with your web designer or other professional if you need help posting audios and/or videos.

Don't Make Things Up

Testimonials are very powerful if they are real and include the customer's first and last names, their company or business, and the city where they live. The two primary types of testimonials are:

- Results-driven
- Feel-good

Results-driven testimonials have more impact: Your product provided a specific result to the person giving you the testimonial.

Three Primary Parts to a Well-Developed Testimonial

- Situation
- Solution
- Result(s)

The situation outlines the problem the customer needed to have solved. The solution is your company. And the results are the increase or decrease to the problem that you helped your client achieve.

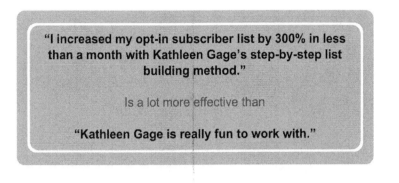

Again, be sure to follow the **FTC guidelines** when using results-driven testimonials. Go to http://www.ftc.gov/opa/2009/10/endortest.shtm to learn more.

Add This for More Credibility

A testimonial containing the customer's name, company, city, and state along with their web or email address is more believable than one with just their initials.

When you first gather testimonials, you may not have particularly powerful statements to use. Simply begin getting in the practice of asking for testimonials. As your experience and success with your customers increase, you can change the testimonials you use.

One success builds on another. As your successes increase, so will the quality of the testimonials you receive.

Pictures

It helps to include a picture of your customer next to their endorsement. This is yet another way to increase its validity.

Use of Name and Testimonial Release

I, _____, give [Company/Organization Name] permission to use my name and comments in the marketing testimonials communication material prepared after my interview with [Interviewer's Name].

Permission is granted to use all or any part of my testimonial as indicated below and to edit the testimonial as [Company/Organization Name] thinks necessary, provided that such editing does not materially change the information or viewpoint I provided.

I understand that I have the opportunity to review my testimonial periodically and to make changes when needed.

Dated: _____

Signature:

_____

Company:

_____

**Reword and rework as needed.

Use Testimonials on Your Website

Placing testimonials on your website can be a very effective use of space. I have a page dedicated solely to testimonials. This allows prospective clients to read what others have to say about their experiences with me. The following two were used with my Amazon.com bestseller training program:

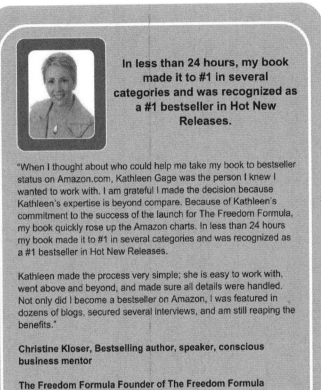

In less than 24 hours, my book made it to #1 in several categories and was recognized as a #1 bestseller in Hot New Releases.

"When I thought about who could help me take my book to bestseller status on Amazon.com, Kathleen Gage was the person I knew I wanted to work with. I am grateful I made the decision because Kathleen's expertise is beyond compare. Because of Kathleen's commitment to the success of the launch for The Freedom Formula, my book quickly rose up the Amazon charts. In less than 24 hours my book made it to #1 in several categories and was recognized as a #1 bestseller in Hot New Releases.

Kathleen made the process very simple; she is easy to work with, went above and beyond, and made sure all details were handled. Not only did I become a bestseller on Amazon, I was featured in dozens of blogs, secured several interviews, and am still reaping the benefits."

Christine Kloser, Bestselling author, speaker, conscious business mentor

The Freedom Formula Founder of The Freedom Formula Experience

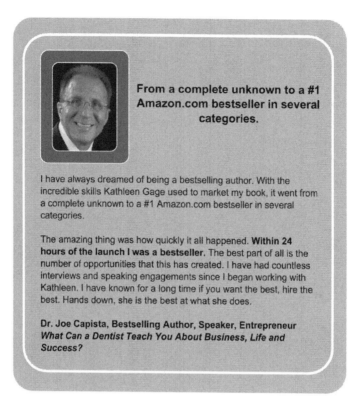

From a complete unknown to a #1 Amazon.com bestseller in several categories.

I have always dreamed of being a bestselling author. With the incredible skills Kathleen Gage used to market my book, it went from a complete unknown to a #1 Amazon.com bestseller in several categories.

The amazing thing was how quickly it all happened. **Within 24 hours of the launch I was a bestseller.** The best part of all is the number of opportunities that this has created. I have had countless interviews and speaking engagements since I began working with Kathleen. I have known for a long time if you want the best, hire the best. Hands down, she is the best at what she does.

Dr. Joe Capista, Bestselling Author, Speaker, Entrepreneur
What Can a Dentist Teach You About Business, Life and Success?

This one used to be posted with my teleseminar training program:

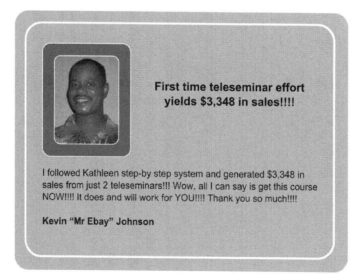

First time teleseminar effort yields $3,348 in sales!!!!

I followed Kathleen step-by step system and generated $3,348 in sales from just 2 teleseminars!!! Wow, all I can say is get this course NOW!!!! It does and will work for YOU!!!! Thank you so much!!!!

Kevin "Mr Ebay" Johnson

This testimonial can be used when I am looking for other media opportunities or to sell a program in which I teach people about working with the media:

> **As the host of a weekly radio show, I always look for guests who can bring a dynamic, entertaining element to my show.**
>
> And, most of the time, that can be a huge challenge, because it's not as easy as many people think. You have to find the right blend of interesting, engaging subject matters presented in a way that keeps the audience from changing the channel. Someone who is able to establish quick rapport with me and my audience is essential. And Kathleen Gage is the epitome of that "perfect" guest. Over the years, I invited her back again and again to my show. I always had complete confidence in her ability and the fact she could and WOULD deliver. She definitely knows what the media wants.
>
> **Charla Haley**
> **On Air Personality**
> **The Breeze Radio Station**
> **Salt Lake City, UT**

Limitations

For some of your customers confidentiality is an issue. Depending on what you helped your customer with, it might be difficult to secure a testimonial with their full name, company, city, and state. In some cases the best you can hope for is a testimonial with a first name and state.

No Paid Experience? No Problem!

If you are just starting out and do not have testimonials from paid customers, you can use testimonials from volunteer work you have done. There is no need to say that you did not get paid for the work done. The purpose of the testimonial is for your colleague to convey their experience of working with you.

As you gain more experience in a given area, you will likely get more testimonials. Update as needed. A very simple way to get a testimonial is to ask. You can also use a simple survey.

Build Your Portfolio Now!

It is never too soon to begin building your portfolio of testimonials and endorsements. The more you have, the more flexibility you have for your online marketing material, your website, and your landing pages.

Chapter 12

Media Releases and Social Media Releases

As a conscious entrepreneur, you want to be on the lookout for as many ways to get your message out as possible. A simple way to gain free publicity and build your opt-in subscriber list is to write and distribute a well-written, well-formatted media release, also known as a press release. It's a very effective yet underutilized publicity tool. There are paid services that will distribute your media releases. If budget is an issue, you can easily find specific locations with a Google search such as "media" in your local market or to a targeted group of people. For example, "where to submit media releases for free" brings up several choices for where to submit a release.

A *media release* is an announcement you distribute to various online locations such as directories, your blog, social networks, and forums. Traditionally press releases were "released" to newspapers and radio and TV stations, and you can do that as well. Public service announcements (PSAs) are also submitted as press releases. Before you write your release, determine:

➻ Your target market
➻ Where your release needs to be viewed and what media outlet serves those locations; for example, a release about a catering service should be directed to a food editor
➻ The contact person at the media outlet (if applicable)
➻ The timeframe for submission
➻ An attention-grabbing headline
➻ The who, what, when, where, why, and how that need to be included
➻ Appropriate quotes, research, and technical data

Social Media Releases

There is ample discussion online as to the "death" of the traditional press release in favor of the social media release (SMR). The SMR is gaining popularity and visibility, and is now viewed by many as a great alternative to the traditional press release.

SMRs are similar to traditional press releases, but they reach people in ways that traditional releases don't.

The purpose of an SMR is to inform the public about your product, build your subscriber list, and drive readers to your landing page where they can opt in for your offering.

SMRs are often linked directly to social networks specific to the market they target. They usually include links to multimedia content at social networks. They focus not only on dissemination of information, but also on the social aspects of the information.

Post your SMR to your blog, ezine, subscriber list, Facebook Fan Page, and the social networks you belong to. You can also post to social media newsrooms. Google "Social Media Newsroom" to learn more.

Be sure to include keywords in the title and text of your release so it will show up in Internet searches. You can also include links that are pertinent to your release information, but if you are using a newsroom or similar service, check to be sure links are not prohibited.

SUPER TIP: An easy way to distribute your SMR is to post the information on your blog. Then post the permalink for your blog with a short bit of information on Twitter, Facebook, and other social networks.

What Method?

The method you use to distribute your media release is determined by your market. If you have a highly wired market, using electronic media is a must and cannot be avoided. If your market is not yet up to speed online, traditional methods that lead them to your website, blog, landing page, or social network are advised.

SMRs are a great choice for bloggers because they can optimize all the features their blog readers are likely to enjoy. You can add audio and/or video for more impact.

The Five Ws of Writing a Media Release

Not long ago I read an article in which the "expert" claimed that it's not necessary to include the five Ws (who, what, when, where, and why) in a media release. Although not absolutely essential in all information you distribute, the five Ws are a great guide to use when developing a release. And most experts agree that including as much information as possible without overdoing it is advisable. To write a power-packed release, include:

- Who is involved – speaker, author, strategist, artist, etc.
- What is taking place
- When it is happening
- Where it will occur
- Why people would be interested in the information

To save a considerable amount of time, create a template for your media releases that can be used over and over. There is no need to reinvent the wheel each time you write one. Write the most important information first. It is not uncommon for media resources to shorten your release, so don't get upset with them for publishing only a portion of it. You don't want to burn bridges with any media source.

Build Relationships

In many cases you will simply submit a media release and hope for the best. This is especially true when you are using electronic formats. But when dealing with someone at a news service, take advantage of the fact that there is a real editor or publisher on the other end of your phone call, email, or fax, and build a relationship with them. (Yes, some people still use fax machines.)

In general it's worth your time to develop relationships with people at newspapers, radio and TV stations, community organizations, and online news services. It's easier to get through gatekeepers if these people know you. This is especially helpful when you promote an event.

When you want to build name recognition in a local market, be sure to include all the local media you can. Small weekly or monthly newspapers and periodicals will often publish a feature story about your business or event if you give them enough lead time. A great way to gain trust and visibility with the media is to provide them with leads about stories that would be of interest to their clientele, even if they are not about your business. This builds a mutually beneficial relationship. Be sure the leads are solid and specific to their market, otherwise you will be viewed as an unreliable source.

Distribution

Many journalists, editors, publishers, and reporters prefer that you send media releases via email. There are also some die-hard snail-mail folks and a few who prefer faxes. Determine their preference and honor their request.

Online publications often require you complete an online form. Be sure to follow their guidelines exactly or your information will not be considered. If you don't find an online submission form, you can send your media release via email within the body of the message as a plain text file – the simpler, the better. Don't send it as an attachment because most media people automatically delete attachments due to concerns about computer viruses.

Don't send a media release to everyone on your media email list using one email with the entire recipient list visible. Individual, personalized emails work better. Keep your message short and sweet; the media is incredibly busy. When an editor calls for more information, respond to their call as quickly and professionally as possible. There is no substitute for building good relationships with the media. Don't ever think you are too busy for them.

Develop Your List of Contacts

Based on what you promote and who your market is, build a list of publications and radio and TV stations along with your contacts there. Concentrate on resources that have readers, listeners, and viewers who fit your target market. Don't waste the time of an editor or producer whose reach is not to those you are targeting.

Show Name	Host	Contact Info	Date Contacted	Result
Business101 www.b101.com	Barbara Tuney	Susan Glow 555-973-4221 s.glow@glow.com	May 10	Will be on show June 11
The Talk www.talk.com	Ellen Fissure	May Hathner 555-667-2211 m.hath@tmt.com	May 12	Will be on show July 2
Sue Torman www.sshow.com	Sue Torman	Tom Dell 555-798-0009 tdell@sshow.com	May 23	Will be on show Oct. 8
In Office www.office.com	Dan Harn	Sally Jones 555-468-2134 sally@office.com	June 3	Will be on show July 7
The Bell www.bells.com	Jay Warner	Jay Warner 555-798-1234 jay@j.warner.com	June 5	Will be on show July 21
Nancy Lee www.nlee.com	Nancy Lee	Sue Jacobs 555-887-9898 sue@sj.com	June 22	Will be on show Aug. 5
Wire News www.wire.com	Dawn Flain	Jan Feller 555-690-8085 jf@wire.com	July 9	Will be on show Aug. 8
The Forty www.forty.com	John Freet	Henry Owen 555-890-6778 owen@howen.com	July 29	Will be on show Aug. 15

The beauty of the Internet is that you can build your list right from the net from plenty of free resource guides. If your market is very targeted, you may have to buy local, regional, national, or international guides that serve targeted audiences.

Another option is paid services such as PRWeb.com or PR.com. Both have great reputations and excellent reach. I have a subscription to PRWeb.com and have received excellent coverage for all the releases I submitted to them. The releases are put on the newswire and on Associated Press distribution channels. Each gets hundreds and often thousands of views by various media channels. All my releases are designed to raise awareness for my products and services and drive traffic to my blog, website, and/or event listings.

So What?

After you write your release, put it aside for at least an hour. Then revisit what you wrote and ask yourself, "So what? Who really cares?" putting yourself in your readers' shoes. If you can't justify a particular phrase in terms of reader interest, leave it out. Have someone else (or several people) read it to make sure you haven't missed anything.

Newsworthy Items for a Media Release

In order to have a great success with your release being selected (especially when submitting to traditional media services), the more newsworthy the subject matter, the better. With SMR you have much more leeway. Below are a few ideas for your subject matter:

- Offering teleseminars or seminars – especially if they are free to the public
- Taking on a leadership role in a professional organization
- A special event open to the public
- A fundraiser
- Recognition in your field
- Special awards
- Release of a book or e-product
- Opening of an exhibit
- Performing an important service to the community

- Running for office
- Inventing, manufacturing, or offering a new product or service
- Being involved in a major news event
- Offering apprenticeships, training programs, classes, or opportunities to volunteer
- Winning a contest, sweepstakes, or lottery
- Opening a business
- Offering franchises of your business

Here are some less newsworthy items that might get published:
- Moving or opening a new branch
- Educational achievements (including attending work-related seminars)
- Hosting an open house
- Hiring or promoting employees
- Annual meetings and conventions

Make It Newsworthy

Your job is to create an interesting piece. Virtually anything can be newsworthy if you search out the *hook*. A hook is a unique angle on a story. There are often several hooks you can use with one announcement, thus turning one release into several.

Controversy

The media loves controversy. A quick view of the evening news or the morning paper will convince you that controversy sells. Is there a controversial angle you can use?

An example of a controversial topic is holding a Pagan gathering in a very conservative Christian region; or lowering the drinking age, texting while driving, or animal testing.

Survey Results

Conduct a survey and create a story around the results. For example, **TRUSTe Releases Survey Results of Parents and Teenagers on Social Networking Behaviors** is a great example of a survey result media release.

Annual Award

Create an annual award for your industry or market and you'll have a newsworthy story each year. This was the subject line of a release for an award I won during the time I was writing this book: **Global Online Marketing Strategist Earns Coveted Suzanne Evans Achievement Award.**

Hot Stuff

Piggyback on something "hot" in the news. Look for opportunities to contact the media when there is a connection between something currently going on and what you have to offer. For example, if there is a sudden spike in gas prices and your company offers close-to-home vacation ideas, that's something the media would take an interest in.

Connect Your Story with a Holiday

Is there a holiday to which your business can link? For example, Martin Luther King Day would be perfect for any company linked to human rights concerns. Gift stores have ample opportunities around Christmas and non-federal holidays like Valentine's Day. Example: **Make Unique Flower Bouquets for Mother's Day with Shakesperry for iPad and iPhone.**

Create a Day

With the popularity of some very unique celebrations such as Cherry Popover Day, Don't Step on a Bee Day, and Hugging Day, why not create your own unique day to address your market's interests and passions?

One client I worked with created a day around the theme of her gift shop. A media release was distributed via several free online resources, and the special day got a lot of online coverage. New customers found her because of this publicity. It didn't cost her anything but time, and she got lots of great coverage shortly after.

Once you decide on the type and name of the special day, let your current customers know, send out a media release, and contact other businesses that might be interested in helping promote it. Here are some examples of days someone decided to bring recognition to:

Love Your Pet Day

Harmony Day

Take Your Daughter to Work Day

Respect Your Elders

Sponsor an Event

The media often feature a company that is involved with a charity event through a sponsorship. Virtually anything can be turned into a story. Your job is to find a way to take the mundane and make it interesting – enough so that the media wants to cover it. Here's an example: **CIOsynergy Announces Brainloop as Official Sponsor for its 2013 Chicago Event.**

Systems Spell Success

As with any aspect of running a business, having systems in place for your marketing and publicity is essential. Develop a system for the writing and distribution of media releases. Stay organized. Know how to send the media release to a specific media outlet and person. Because each has a preference for how they want to receive the release, it will be to your benefit to find out. A quick phone call or email often provides you with this important information.

Editors are inundated with information. To get their attention, keep the release short and to the point. During busy times, like before a huge event in a city, they experience information overload, so be conscious of your timing.

Don't use lots of buzzwords such as *it's all-new, interactive, interoperable, cross-platform,* and *new multimedia solution.* Avoid jargon and acronyms people outside of your industry won't understand. The general public will have no idea what your industry jargon means and editors rarely take the time to find out.

Extras to Enhance Your Social Media Release

You can add any of the following elements to the five Ws discussed previously to substantially increase your viewer's attention span:

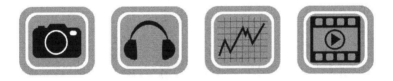

Traditional (offline) media sources search the Internet for stories, so do what you can to effectively use all that is available through the Internet. With the number of online locations that are in constant need of information, it is very easy to gain visibility with online niche media sources.

Internet Media

Over the past few years, *Internet-only* resources have been cropping up. The challenge is deciding where to focus your attention. Once you begin to raise people's awareness about you, your product, and what you stand for, media opportunities for interviews, co-authoring books, telesummits, websummits, and any number of joint-venture projects show up on a fairly regular basis.

Initially this is all very exciting, but you will reach a point where you have to pick and choose very wisely to stay true to your vision, mission, and purpose.

Finding Opportunities

Social network sites such as Facebook, Twitter, LinkedIn, and others like these are great places to search out online media sources. It's just a matter of taking the time and effort to do so.

I have gotten lots of great opportunities with people I found online through social networks who wanted to interview an expert with my background. I have been invited to write articles, reviews, and much more by people who approached me due to my excellent visibility and my proactive approach on social networks.

You might be discovered by a potential joint-venture partner, invited to affiliate campaigns, asked to write articles as a featured expert for a high-traffic blog, or noticed by top experts in your industry. These are just a few of the hidden opportunities you can achieve through increasing your visibility.

Be in the Know

It's obvious that the more you target the media, the more you learn how to work with them. Don't be passed up for great opportunities because you don't know how to approach the media.

In a recent episode of *The Voice*, the final eight contestants were invited to be guests on Carson Daly's radio show. Carson is the host of *The Voice* and a big deal in radio. He told the contestants he wanted them to sing their name and the name of the team they were on. One contestant said in shock, "Are you serious?"

Wow! I was blown away by this. Here the contestant is vying for a million dollars along with celebrity status, and he questioned this amazing opportunity. Rather than shy away, he could have really shined and let his personality come out. When an opportunity like this shows up for you, jump at the chance to shine. Sure it might be a bit nerve-racking, but the more you do it, the better you get and the more fun it becomes.

The way I feel about opportunities that show up is this: If my palms are not sweaty, I'm not playing big enough.

Create Value

If you create a lot of value for the media, you can become an in-demand media contact. Discover what they want and be alert to opportunity. To learn what they want:

➸ Read what they write
➸ Watch their programs
➸ Follow their tweets
➸ Hook up on various social networks
➸ Know the genre
➸ Ask

Be an Avid Media Watcher

Whether you work with online or offline media sources, it is critical to become familiar with them before your initial contact, especially if you hope to have a feature story written, secure an interview, or write a guest column. Research past postings, stories, and articles written or edited by your contact. A simple Google search can pull up this information.

Be Appreciative

It's always a great idea to thank anyone who features you, interviews you, or writes about you, but there are strict rules in some environments. A simple thank you card is appropriate and welcome (and a long-lost art). Although it may seem harmless, sending gifts is sometimes strictly forbidden, especially with traditional media sources. Besides, they would rather have a good hook than a gift.

Online media can be very, very different. I have often sent a thank you gift to a show host or a blog owner. Usually it is one of my books or something relatively inexpensive, and these gifts have been well-received.

Provide Requested Information

Follow up on what you promised. Get back to a reporter, journalist, show host, or blog owner even if you don't have the information they requested. Do everything possible to avoid being late. If there will be a delay, let them know what is going on and the reason for any holdup. They have deadlines just like you do – more crucial ones in many cases.

The more reliable you are, the more likely they are to want to work with you again, and the more likely they will refer you to colleagues who may be in need of interviewing someone of your caliber. Do all you can to make their job easy.

You're Not that Memorable

Although we would like to think so, someone who has interviewed us or written or published a story about us may not instantly recall who we are. Don't assume that those you have contacted from the media will remember you from one contact. They are extremely busy, and the easier you make their job, the more you will be noticed and be remembered.

Be Consistent

People who get a lot of visibility from both online and offline resources don't let up on their media marketing. Include it in your overall marketing plan.

Working with Reporters

Reporters work on unforgiving deadlines. When a reporter calls you, always find out what deadline they are facing, and return their call as quickly as possible.

Ask for the reporter's name and the media organization for which they are reporting. It's best not to play favorites when deciding whether or not to grant an interview to a specific reporter; it may come back to haunt you.

When a reporter calls requesting an interview, you have a right to ask what the topic will be and for some sample questions. If you need time to collect your thoughts and the reporter's deadline allows, offer to call back later at a specific time, and follow through. Reporters' schedules are determined by the breaking news of the day, so don't get upset if an interview gets canceled or rescheduled because a more urgent story arises.

Rarely will you be able to review a story before it goes to press. Years ago I wrote a monthly column for *The Enterprise*, a business journal based in Utah. Occasionally I included information about local businesspeople. I never let them review my columns, because they might have wanted to change too much or make me miss my deadline. If that wasn't acceptable to them, I wouldn't include them in the column.

What not to do when dealing with the media:

- Don't be full of yourself.
- Don't miss a deadline.
- Don't call your contacts on deadline dates.
- Don't become passive; working with the media is an ongoing process.
- Don't ask to see a piece before it goes to print.

When Your Release Is Published, Blog It

Posting your media release to your blog is a very effective marketing strategy. If you have written your release using keywords, adding it to your blog increases SEO.

Backend Opportunities

Gaining as much traction as possible through a media release takes time. In addition to where it initially appears, there are many other ways to reach even more potential viewers of the release. These are called *backend* opportunities.

Once your media release is published, you can tweet the permalink and post something about the release on your Facebook wall or to your Fans, with the permalink in the post.

Years ago I partnered with four colleagues on an event called "The Radiant Success Event." Not only did the five coordinators post the media release to various online locations, we blogged about it, tweeted the permalink, posted it on our Facebook walls, announced it at other social networks and media sources, and included it in announcements to our opt-in subscribers.

Set Up a Media Room on Your Blog or Website

A media room contains key information the media would need from you. It can include other media releases, your bio, photos they can use with a story about you, podcasts (if applicable), links to interviews, etc.

Monitor What Shows Up

It's important to know what is showing up online about you, your industry, your product, or anything else that is relevant to you. One of the simplest ways to do this is to register with **Google Alert** and **Yahoo Alert**. These are free services that alert you when something you have asked to be notified about shows up.

To set up an alert, go to Google and key in "Google Alert." Follow the steps. Do the same at Yahoo using "Yahoo Alert." Although you won't be alerted about everything online about you, it's a great way to track your media-release coverage, articles, posts you are mentioned in, and other visibility-building resources.

The goal of media releases is to gain visibility. The more visibility you get, the more likely it is you will be contacted by various media outlets. News releases often result in interviews, which can lead to even more news release opportunities. Remember, the way to get massive online visibility is to know how to create a great hook, be very consistent in your marketing and promotions, and be very easy to work with when the media contacts you.

Give Full Permission

To make it very easy for media contacts to use your information, add a statement to your release that gives them full permission to use your information.

Gain Recognition as an Authority

The more the media views you as an authority, the more likely they will consult you in the future. Keep up with your media outreach efforts to help establish you as an authority or expert.

Chapter 13

The Power and Profit of Free Publicity

I believe in equality for everyone, except reporters and photographers.
—Mohandas Gandhi

The beauty of the Internet is the vast choices available for marketing and promoting to gain massive visibility. There are paid opportunities and free opportunities; free opportunities are known as *organic publicity*.

In all the years I have been successfully marketing, both online and offline, I have gotten most of my traffic and publicity, which often work hand in hand, organically. There are ample opportunities if you keep your eyes and ears open. Many people make a feeble or one-time attempt at gaining publicity, and when they don't immediately get massive coverage, they give up, concluding that they have to hire an expensive public relations (PR) firm to do the job.

For most solopreneurs, hiring a PR firm is cost-prohibitive. You can pay thousands of dollars a month with no guarantee of good results. I highly recommend you learn the fundamentals of publicity so you can do it yourself and outsource portions if necessary. There are plenty of virtual assistants and social media experts who can help. You can get literally thousands, tens of thousands, and even hundreds of thousands of dollars' worth of free publicity through your own efforts if you know what you're doing.

Years ago I partnered with *New York Times* bestselling author Dian Thomas, who secured millions of dollars of free publicity at the peak of her career as an author. Dian developed a program about how to secure lots of free publicity, and I was the promotions director for the live events she hosted.

With event after event we used the very same free publicity strategies that Dian taught. I had been using them in my own business for years, and it was a true delight to partner with someone who also understood how powerful free publicity is. And with all the rooms we filled with those eager to learn our secrets, it was very, very profitable for us. It's truly a pity that more people don't seek out organic publicity, because it can increase your credibility and profit margins substantially.

Types of Publicity

Publicity primarily comes from two sources – traditional media and electronic media.

Traditional media:
- Radio
- Television
- Print newspapers
- Magazines
- Trade journals
- Print newsletters such as company and association newsletters

Electronic media:
- Press directories
- Online magazines
- Internet radio
- Online newspapers
- Online trade journals
- Forums
- Blogs
- Social networks
- Email discussion groups
- Ezines

With the popularity of the Internet, many people are bypassing or overlooking the power of traditional media. Not everyone is wired, and you should capture that huge part of your potential market. And many people find what is available on the Internet through articles, newsletters, radio, and TV. You can gain incredible publicity online, but by driving traffic to the Internet through offline publicity, you can greatly increase your online audience.

Many reporters, journalists, editors, and producers of traditional media find story ideas and experts to interview via social networks, online article directories, blogs, blog carnivals, and any number of other avenues available on the Internet. So a combination of both electronic and traditional methods is likely to produce the best results. Of course, if your market is highly wired, using electronic media is a must and cannot be avoided.

Keep the Fires Burning

Gaining publicity should be an ongoing goal for you and your business. It is not a one-time deal even though many treat it as such. *Constantly fuel the media fire!* Find hot areas of interest that the media wants to cover. With the right plan, systems, and vision, you can immediately gain publicity and continually tap in to its power for years to come.

Understand What's Unique about Various Media Sources

Each media source is looking for something specific for their audience. Your job is to present your information in a way that is appealing to the medium you are targeting.

Newspapers

Newspapers often attract an older readership. They are designed to be information-based. Use them to educate and inform through articles, feature stories, and media releases.

Television

Because TV is so visual, your pitch must capture the viewer's interest. With so much channel-surfing going on, you have to grab your viewer's attention quickly. Don't rely on your producer to figure out what will grab their attention; convey your message clearly to secure TV opportunities.

Publicity Targets

Make a list of all the avenues you will use to gain publicity. An online search will bring up ample resources. Add to your list specific departments, editors, and producers to contact.

Publicity Calendar

Planning your publicity campaign increases your chances for success. Create a timetable to ensure that you stay on target and keep your name in front of the media on a regular basis.

Tie your campaign to special holidays and unique events. Always look for the hook in your story – what makes your event, idea, information product, book, or presentation unique.

Radio

Now on to some really fun stuff – if you relax and enjoy yourself! It applies to traditional radio and Internet radio, known as *Web radio*. Not only can you be a featured expert on a radio program, but you can also start your own radio program.

Radio is an excellent medium to optimize your personality. When being interviewed, keep the conversation going and present interesting content. If you are uncomfortable about being interviewed, get media coaching. It is an invaluable investment of time and money.

Lots of people are extremely intimidated by the thought of going on air, but when you consider what it can open up for you, it might be time to walk through your fear. You have a message to get out to the world. When you keep this in the forefront of your thinking, speaking on the air becomes much easier. A good coach can help you address your fears, polish your presentation style, and shine. Those who are skilled at the interview process were not born that way. The more you practice, the better you get, and radio presentation is no exception.

In the past two decades I have been interviewed hundreds of times on radio, in teleseminars and webinars, and at conferences, but I wasn't always comfortable about speaking in public. I was often too concerned about things being perfect, setting myself up for failure, or coming across as nervous. With time and experience these things became nonissues.

An interview is simply a conversation. The more relaxed you

are, the more natural the conversation and the more you can be yourself. The more you are yourself, the more people will like you for who you are.

Radio is a great vehicle for increasing the market's perception of you as an expert, and hosts are always in need of entertaining and informative guests. An advantage of web radio is that when your show information is posted, you gain Google ranking. And a podcast of the show can be posted on the radio-show website, so your interview can continue to attract attention for a long time. You never know how many opportunities will show up after a great interview.

I used to fear a host trying to stump me. That has proven to be an unfounded fear. There are very few Howard Stern types in the world. In most cases, a host wants you have a great interview because when *you* do a good job, *they* succeed in the audience's ears. Rarely does a host come from an adversarial position unless what you are talking about is extremely controversial. Even when that is the case, you can still come across as professional and create an incredible opportunity for you and your business or cause.

From the Comfort of Your Home

When I first started in radio it was necessary to record programs at a studio. Today radio is such that you can conduct most interviews over the phone regardless of whether they are for traditional radio or Internet radio. I have had occasion to do as many as five interviews in a day from my home office. In between interviews I took my dogs for walks, worked on other projects, or just took time to regroup.

I'm not recommending you go from zero to five in a day, but just know that the number of interviews you can set up is unlimited. If you are promoting a book, an event, or a new information product, radio is a great marketing strategy.

Be a *Star* Radio Guest

Think on your feet when being interviewed (and when conducting an interview). Radio is a mix of news and entertainment, and though you're not expected to act like a seasoned entertainer, you should think in terms of how to engage your audience.

Great radio guests are not easy to find. Treat a radio interview as a great opportunity, because it is. When word gets around that you do a great interview, lots more opportunities will likely show up. There were several occasions when I finished an interview and within minutes received an email requesting an interview from someone who had been listening. Here are some simple tips to help you shine:

➥ Provide the information the host needs as soon as possible.

➥ Prepare a short bio to send to the host.

➥ Prepare a selection of questions.

➥ Avoid using jargon most people won't understand. Unless it is a technical show, talk in basics.

➥ Be brief with your answers. Practice so you know what main points to address.

➥ If you are being interviewed about a book you wrote, don't expect a show host to have read your whole book, and don't be offended when they haven't. But *you* need to know your book very well, as they may ask questions about specific information in your book.

➥ Don't use a cell phone when being interviewed remotely unless this is absolutely your only option.

➥ Use a conversational tone. Be engaging. Be entertaining.

➥ When there is dead air time (silence), immediately pick up the slack. Even a short period of silence is a no-no in the radio world.

➥ Invest in a media coach if you are not a seasoned show guest.

➥ You are being interviewed to inform, educate, entertain, or inspire. The producer doesn't care about anything but that.

However, if you make arrangements ahead of time, you may be able to promote your product.

➡ Speak clearly.

➡ Pace yourself.

➡ Avoid background noise. It is essential to control the background noise during a call. Too many distractions can literally ruin your interview.

>> Make sure you are using a quiet location.

>> Let others in your home know you are recording a session.

>> Close doors and windows.

>> Get dogs and children out of earshot.

>> Mute all other phones within earshot.

>> Don't check email while you are on the call.

➡ After the interview, send the host a thank you card or letter.

Finding Opportunities

Okay, so you're ready to get "on the air." Now what? There are a number of ways to find more than enough shows in need of experts to interview. It's simply a matter of investing some time in the process.

Keep in mind that different shows address different areas of interest. As with any part of your marketing, finding the right match is essential. For example, there would be no point in contacting a radio host who is seeking guests who specialize in parenting topics if you specialize in growing a business. And let's say you have a very liberal outlook on spirituality; contacting conservative religious programs would not do you or the host any good.

The more focused you are on looking for a good match, the easier the process will be and the less time will be wasted chasing after the wrong opportunity. Take time to think about all the types of shows for which your area of expertise would be a great match.

Google Search

Whatever your area of expertise, there are bound to be plenty of shows you can be a guest on. With online radio the opportunities are endless. There are several platforms to choose from. One of the most popular platforms is BlogTalk Radio, which calls itself a *social radio network*. There are shows of every description there, and hosts who are always in need of guests. Not all shows are necessarily a good use of your time, but if you are just adding this to your marketing mix, go for as many shows as possible.

The challenge with BlogTalk is that you can run into unseasoned hosts. A great majority of the shows do not have live listeners, but the downloads can be incredible. You have to determine, based on your goals, if it's worth your effort. A few years ago I had a BlogTalk radio show. Although I had few live listeners, thousands downloaded the show every week.

To find shows, do a Google search with the words "Internet radio programs + [your topic]" to bring up ample shows. This approach can be very time-consuming. You may want to hire a virtual assistant who can help with the logistics of setting up interviews. There are plenty of virtual assistants who offer this type of service.

Finding Hosts via Social Networks

It's likely you have connections, friends, followers, and subscribers at your various social networks who are show hosts. Sometimes all it takes is to search on keywords to locate specific profiles. If you are actively involved in social networks and your expertise is well-positioned, there's a great chance hosts will contact you.

Media guides provide listings of stations in your market. They usually include the producers, editors, and publishers, and their contact information, which saves you lots of time locating the right contacts. Virtually every market has a media guide you can either purchase or rent. A Google search will give you ample choices.

When you find a fit, get yourself booked immediately. Take full advantage of these opportunities. They are plentiful, and they definitely increase your market position, visibility, and expert status. Keep "your big why" at the forefront of all you are doing. When you keep this in mind, everything should fall into place. That's not to say it won't take work, because it will. But your why helps you to get through times of frustration when it seems you may be working too hard for the results you are experiencing.

Host Your Own Show

Does the thought of your own radio program appeal to you? New shows are cropping up every single day, and there are ample opportunities to create your own show, especially with Internet-based programs. Depending on availability of airtime, you can often start a program at little or no expense. Some online platforms require you to pay for the airtime. If you don't have the budget for that, you can sell advertising or secure sponsors.

When you first start your program it may be difficult to secure sponsors and advertisers unless you have a solid marketing plan in place. If they are going to invest money in you, they need to know there will be a return on their investment. The number one way to convince someone to part with their money is to prove you have listeners, so do whatever you can to increase your listenership.

You have likely noticed that throughout *Power Up for Profits* everything is driven by marketing and promotions. No two ways about it – you have to market. If you plan to sell advertising time, I recommend you hire a sales professional rather than doing it yourself. This frees up your time and focus for your show. You can pay a flat rate, which I don't recommend; you can pay a base rate plus commission; or you can pay a commission only.

If your show is about interviewing guests, you of course will need to line up guests. Make sure you have engaging guests or your show may not attract listeners or viewers. You can actually do a lot to position your expert status by interviewing high-profile guests. As with advertisers and sponsors, the more you can show you have a strong listenership, the greater your chances of attracting high-profile guests for your show.

With a long-term vision you can easily turn radio guests into event guests for a telesummit or websummit. A *websummit* is an online event that brings together a group of experts who share their expertise as part of the group. A websummit differs from a webinar in that a webinar usually features just one expert, and a websummit involves many experts.

As you grow your business, think in terms of connecting all these ideas together. How can one activity lead to another and another and another?

Let the World Know

Starting a radio program is the easy part. Next comes the fun of getting the word out. The more listeners you have, the more backend opportunities you have. If you can stand apart from the crowd, the opportunities are endless.

You can promote your show by way of media releases, through social networks, in forums, on your blog, and through articles, your website, and joint-venture partners. It takes more than securing great interviews to gain the most out of the opportunity. Think in terms of win/win.

The win for the listeners is simply to give them a great experience so that the time they take away from other activities is well invested. The win for you is that your show is an opportunity to reach new listeners (potential customers).

Preparing for a Radio Interview

As you pursue broadcast media opportunities, the more prepared you are, the better. When you receive an invitation to be a featured expert on a show, response time is essential, so have the following promotional material ready for immediate delivery to your host:

→ Bio
→ Headshot or photo that is appropriate for the show
→ Topic(s)
→ Introduction (keep this short)
→ Questions
→ Promotional information including media release(s), tweets, and landing-page content.

Bio

Your bio outlines your expertise, experience, and other relevant information.

Headshot

Yes, you do need a headshot for an online radio engagement; access is through the visual Internet. Use a picture that portrays the image you wish to convey in relation to the show.

Topics

A list of topics from which the host can select is a very welcome addition to your promotional material. Choose the topics with which you want to be identified.

Sometimes hosts want me to talk about something I am qualified to talk about, but the topic is not what I deal with currently. For example, years ago I did a great deal of work with trade-show management. Although I am very qualified to speak on the topic, it is not a service I offer today. Rather than using an hour of time to talk about this, it is better to either decline the opportunity or encourage the host to interview me about my present focus.

Introduction

An introduction is different from a bio. Although there may be some of the same information in each, an introduction is usually much shorter and in a more conversational tone than a bio. Be sure to clarify which is to be used when you are introduced on the air. Once my host took it upon herself to take a bunch of information off my website, and spent more than five minutes introducing me. The longer she went on, the more uncomfortable I became. Not only did the introduction sound extremely boastful, it definitely cut into our interview time.

Bio

Kathleen Gage is the "no-nonsense, common sense" speaker, author, and product-creation specialist, and owner of the highly successful company, Power Up For Profits. Kathleen helps entrepreneurs make money online. Kathleen's clients are driven by making a difference through their own unique voice.

Considered to be one of the nation's most passionate speakers, Kathleen is known for cutting through the fluff and helping people leave their sob stories behind so they can stop focusing on the past and start looking toward the future. She speaks and teaches about what she believes are the core elements of a successful life: accountability, integrity, honesty, and living with passion and hope.

This is not to say that Kathleen doesn't know struggle. At the age of twenty-five she was homeless without a college degree. With no direction, no focus, and no true purpose, she wondered if she'd ever find a use for her life. Following a spiritual awakening, she decided it was time to do something with her life and "come out of hiding." This started an upward trajectory over thirty years ago that led to the creation of her first company, Street Smarts Marketing, in 1994.

Since then Kathleen has become a much sought-after speaker and writer, refusing to deliver what she calls "boring-ass messages." Her mission is to help people understand that their business is merely a means to get their message out to the world. She teaches that it's not just about what you do, but the reasons behind why you do it.

When Kathleen speaks, people listen. And when you see on her stage, you will leave excited, inspired, and ready to step into your own greatness.

Introduction for a Show on Product Creation

If you've been online for any length of time, you've heard that there are people making great money with information products – people making six figures and above. Not only can you make great money by packaging your knowledge, you're also able to impact a global market.

There's just one problem; lots of people aren't quite sure where to start with product creation. Do they start with an ebook, home study course, teleseminar, webinar, MP3, or what?

If you don't know what to do, you can waste a lot of money and time spinning your wheels. One person who does know how to create profitable and in-demand products is Kathleen Gage. Kathleen is a globally recognized expert in the world of product creation. She teaches experts in virtually every industry how to package their knowledge into money-making products and services. As you will see, she takes the complex and shows you how you can get products to market fast, effectively, and profitably.

I'm thrilled to have Kathleen here today to share with you the fastest way for you to get your products to market.

Welcome Kathleen....

Recommended Questions

In the great majority of interviews I have done, the hosts welcome any questions I can provide prior to the show. Only once or twice have I been interviewed by someone who wanted to "surprise" me with questions.

On a couple of occasions a host wanted me to script out the entire interview (or worse yet, the host wanted to script it). I don't like working off scripts. I usually take along a few notes to refer to, but spontaneity is sacrificed when you read from a script. I tried using one once – it was an awful experience. I now decline such interviews because they inhibit my interview style. Remember, your interview is a conversation. You don't script conversations (hopefully you don't), so don't script interviews.

The best interviews are those that have a structure *and* a conversational quality. This is why providing questions is helpful, but don't be so attached to the questions that when the host asks something other than what you provided you are at a loss as to what to say. I always let the host know I am completely open to spontaneous questions in addition to those I provide.

Marketing Tools

Make the job of the host as easy as possible when it comes to promoting your show. The number one thing you can do is provide ample information to be used in promotions. There are a few reasons why I like to provide promotional material to a host. One, it makes their job easier. Two, promotions get started sooner. Three, some hosts don't have the time or resources to develop the material. And four, I know my material best. I have various versions of my promotional material and prefer to choose what is most appropriate to the show. The longer you have been doing interviews, the less time it takes to customize material for a particular appearance. If you don't have time to do this, hire a virtual assistant to handle the details. It will pay off in the long run. Here are some promotional materials you can provide:

➤➤ **Tweets**

I recommend writing at least twenty tweets to post to your Twitter account for each show, as well as twenty to send to your host if they request tweets.

➤ **Social Network Postings**

Provide a few short postings of one or two paragraphs for Facebook, Google+, LinkedIn, and other applicable social networks.

➤ **Calendars**

Give the *who, what, when, where,* and *why* to be posted on various online calendars.

➤ **Media Release**

As with tweets, you can write a media release for your own promotions as well as providing one for the host.

➤ **Overview of Topic Information**

I also recommend providing a topic overview in addition to the individual items listed above, though very few guests do so. Include the topic you and the host have decided on, a few insights about the topic to orient your host, benefits for the listener, a shortened version of your bio, your introduction, and a headshot.

Secure the Gig

When I am promoting a book or new product, I like to incorporate web radio to gain massive visibility for the launch. Even if I can't overtly promote my new release on a particular show, when I do a great job with the interview my web traffic increases. When my website is optimized, I am prepared for this spike in visitors. Everything you do online is connected.

On occasion hosts want to become affiliates for the product I'm launching. It's a good idea to mention such an opportunity to your host and let them decide whether it's a fit for their business model.

It is very important that you stay organized regarding:

➤ Recording the dates of your contacts with the host and show representative

➤ What information you send and when:
  » Bio
  » Photo
  » Topic

» Introduction
» Questions
» Promotional information
» Overview
» Contact information including email address, cell phone, and office phone
» Other
➤ When you need to follow up
➤ What promotions you have done and will do

A simple form like the one below can help you stay on track.

Show Name	Host	Contact Info	Date Contacted	Result
Business101 www.b101.com	Barbara Tuney	Susan Glow 555-973-4221 s.glow@glow.com	May 10	Will be on show June 11
The Talk www.talk.com	Ellen Fissure	May Hathner 555-667-2211 m.hath@tmt.com	May 12	Will be on show July 2
Sue Torman www.sshow.com	Sue Torman	Tom Dell 555-798-0009 tdell@sshow.com	May 23	Will be on show Oct. 8
In Office www.office.com	Dan Harn	Sally Jones 555-468-2134 sally@office.com	June 3	Will be on show July 7
The Bell www.bells.com	Jay Warner	Jay Warner 555-798-1234 jay@j.warner.com	June 5	Will be on show July 21
Nancy Lee www.nlee.com	Nancy Lee	Sue Jacobs 555-887-9898 sue@sj.com	June 22	Will be on show Aug. 5
Wire News www.wire.com	Dawn Flain	Jan Feller 555-690-8085 jf@wire.com	July 9	Will be on show Aug. 8
The Forty www.forty.com	John Freet	Henry Owen 555-890-6778 owen@howen.com	July 29	Will be on show Aug. 15

When I first began to book interview opportunities, I booked all my own shows. I now have a project manager who handles my bookings. Although the process outlined below can be used for virtually any platform, the information is specific to BlogTalk Radio.

➻ Go to http://www.blogtalkradio.com. Search for programs using your keywords. What are the keywords people use to search for your product? These are the same words to use to find a show. There are shows for every market and topic.

➻ Go to the show page. I did a search with the word "dogs." Several choices came up.

➻ Review the show information to ensure it's a good fit for your topic. Don't assume it is a good fit until you do a bit of research. Notice what past segments were about and who some of the guests have been.

➻ To get a great sense of whether or not the show is a good fit for you, listen to portions of past shows. This will inform you about the skill level of the host and how easily conversations flow.

➻ Create a BlogTalk profile. You don't need to have a show to have a profile. The profile allows you access to shows on BlogTalk. Each format is different. Simply read the "help" section if needed.

➻ Add the show or show host to your Twitter and Facebook friends using the links on the page.

➻ When requesting them as a Facebook friend, send them a message explaining that you came across their BlogTalk show and appreciate their content. This is a great rule of thumb whenever you are inviting someone to be your friend on Facebook.

➻ In BlogTalk, look for their website and email address so you have an even better idea of who they are and what else they do besides BlogTalk Radio. The email address is always good to have on file for yet another way to contact the host.

➤ Send a short, personal email inquiring about their need for guest experts. If you can't find their personal email address, you can send it via BlogTalk's messaging feature. In many cases you can contact a host through the more widely used social networks like Facebook and LinkedIn. In your inquiry letter:

   » Refer to their show by name.
   » Reference a particular show you listened to.
   » Reference who referred you (if that's the case).
   » State how you discovered their show.
   » Introduce yourself and your topic, and provide a short description of your topic.
   » Attach a speaker sheet (or better, a link to an online PDF of your speaker sheet). A speaker sheet is a short document that lists a speaker's major credits and gives a brief history of their career. In essence, it is a bio.
   » Provide a link to your website and/or blog.
   » Thank them for their consideration and time.

Keep it short and to the point – your speaker sheet will provide the details.

➤ Follow up in one week.

Time-Savers

➤ Add a radio-host list to your Twitter and Facebook accounts. As you come across shows of interest, add them to your list for future reference.

➤ Listen to shows you like. You will show up on their BlogTalk page as a listener.

➤ Familiarize yourself with colleagues' shows.

It's amazing how quickly you can build name recognition when you have a very focused approach to securing radio interviews. Imagine what type of results you could get if you appeared on the air – two or three times a week for a year.

Chapter 14

Teleseminars and Webinars

As the Internet has become more and more popular, so have training methods that don't require leaving the comfort of your home or office. *Teleseminars* – seminars conducted by phone, also known as *teleconferences, teleclasses,* and *telecoaching,* initially were more readily embraced by home-based entrepreneurs because they cost so little to host.

Early on, not only the cost of hosting a webinar but also the lack of service providers for small and solo businesses were prohibitive for many people. But as demand grew, so did the number of choices available for the market. Both teleseminars and webinars allow you to facilitate a training session with participants from around the globe as long as you have a phone, a computer, and an Internet connection.

It was in the late nineties that I discovered the power and profit of teleseminars. In the last fifteen years I've made a lot of money, gained market reach, increased my subscriber numbers, and created various information products with teleseminars.

In 2010 I hosted my first webinar. I actually resisted webinars for several years because I was having so much success with teleseminars. When I discovered the potential of webinars, I had to wonder why I waited so long to make them part of my marketing strategy.

The first teleseminar I hosted was not very successful at all; only fifty people registered. But I knew nothing about making enticing offers to increase my revenues. Today my teleseminars always attract several hundred registrants and sometimes into the thousands.

In the early days of teleseminars, if 100 people registered, close to 100 people showed up. At the time of this writing, the numbers of people who show up can be as low as 10 percent of registrants, with an average of 30 to 40 percent. This is because people have grown accustomed to receiving the replay of the event.

Paid programs are a completely different story. For the purposes of *Power Up for Profits*, teleseminars and webinars are yet another way to build your visibility, expert status, and subscriber list.

Teleseminars

Conducting teleseminars, also known as group learning conference calls, which describes exactly what they are, is a very effective strategy for promoting your small business or professional practice and creating additional streams of income. They are a very versatile and efficient way to deliver your services and build your business. The great news is that they are very easy to set up and record, once you know how, and profit margins are extremely high.

Here are some ideas to jumpstart your creative thinking for delivering your own seminars over the phone:

- Hosting free teleseminars is a great way to promote your business and let new prospects get to know you.

- Teleseminars provide opportunities to collaborate and do joint ventures with other people who already have a good subscriber list, in order to gain exposure to new prospects and grow your own list.

- If you're just starting out, teleseminars are a great format for interviewing top experts in your niche, recording these interviews, providing replays as a bonus for signing up for your newsletter, or packaging them as a product. Granted, you can simply record a conversation with an expert and offer it as a replay, but by hosting a teleseminar that others can listen to, you create frontend and backend opportunities.

- Position yourself as the expert in your field by developing and delivering great content in your specialty area for your teleseminar. Teach what you know and love while increasing your visibility and gaining valuable exposure and credibility. This reinforces your brand and gives people a low-cost way to get to know you.

- Attract participants and fill your teleseminars by finding affiliate partners to help you with promotion. Collaborating with an affiliate to offer learning opportunities is a very effective and inexpensive way to get more listeners, increase your market reach, and position your expert status through a third-party endorsement.

➺ Have your teleseminars transcribed and offer your customers a transcript of the call. By bundling the replay and the transcripts, you create higher perceived value. This can substantially increase your profits with minimal additional expense.

➺ You can charge as much for a teleseminar as you would for a workshop while saving travel time, travel costs, and venue costs, and it's easier and cheaper to get people to register.

➺ You can leverage teleseminars by turning them into products and multiple streams of income. Use teleseminars to create an information empire of content – ebooks, workbooks, CDs, products, and multi-media courses. The same information can be repackaged and reproduced in several different platforms to generate extra income.

➺ Include affiliate programs and hyperlinks for sites you mention during your teleseminar. Send an automated email out after the class that includes these links to generate affiliate income.

➺ The key to profitable teleseminars is that *the fortune is in the follow-up.* You can make *upsells* after people order your teleseminar by offering the transcript afterward for a minimal extra charge rather than bundling it in the original price, or by creating a backend program to add to your sales funnel and make much more income than from the one teleseminar alone.

A little-known secret for converting visitors to your sites into paying teleseminar customers is to satisfy the "try before you buy" mentality. Debbi Fields, founder of Mrs. Field's Cookies, was a master at this. When she first began her business, no one believed she would succeed. Even though her husband's business acquaintances loved her cookies, when she asked them about starting a cookie business none of them thought it was a good idea. "Bad idea," they said with their mouths stuffed full of cookies; "Give it up, there's no way." Debbi's mother, in-laws, friends, and fellow students at Los Altos Junior College all said she would fail.

Against all odds, Debbi signed a lease for her first cookie store in Palo Alto, California, on August 18, 1977. She opened her store at 9:00 a.m., but by noon nobody had bought even one cookie. Frustrated, but not ready to give up, she took samples to people on the streets. They liked the samples so much that many of them returned to actually buy cookies. Providing free samples to potential customers remained a cornerstone of her business in the years to come. Imagine that. Almost everyone thought she would fail, but by offering samples, she built an empire.

The same principle holds true for you. Before you launch into trying to sell potential customers who might know very little about you or your product, give them a "taste"; offer a preview teleseminar.

One client I worked with was struggling to make money in her business. She was barely getting by when she decided to hire me as her mentor. What she had working in her favor was a very solid market reach, a clearly defined market, and that she is one of the most highly respected experts in her market. She has a very spiritually conscious market who love and adore her, yet sales were not at all what she wanted or needed to keep her business profitable.

The solution we worked on was a series of preview teleseminars that led to a $4,000 program available to only twenty-five people. The result: hundreds of people in her preview calls, and all twenty-five spots for the special program filled within a very short period of time. Not only did she make a substantial amount of money with this formula, she gained hundreds more potential customers.

Keep this story in mind as you develop your teleseminars. It's not what you do in the short term that matters, but the long-term potential. Once people are on your subscriber list, there is unlimited opportunity available to you.

Holding live workshops and seminars is a good way to build a business, but securing a venue and audio-visual aids and providing refreshments for the participants make such events quite expensive, and there are many factors that can prevent them from being successful and profitable, not to mention that it's costly for attendees to travel to them.

Events, when done correctly, can be very, very profitable, but the financial risk is much higher, too. This is why businesses are more often choosing teleseminars for their workshops and training sessions. All the attendees have to do is dial in to the conference line or click on a website URL. The cost is fairly reasonable. I have made tens of thousands of dollars on several occasions with an investment of $50 to $100. Participants like them because they can join in from anywhere in the world without having to travel. If the teleseminar is recorded, they can listen at their leisure.

Teleseminars are a unique route to building a business. You can use them to demonstrate how to use a product, conduct training, hold group coaching sessions, answer questions or provide tips about a product or your business, recruit people, and generate leads. And reaching a global market costs you no more than reaching a regional market.

Before rushing to hold a teleseminar, make sure you have a long-term plan in place for building your business and your reputation as an expert. Here's a very simple strategy: Hold a teleseminar each month to offer help and advice and disseminate valuable information that is of interest to your current and prospective customers. Offer valuable knowledge and insights. Once people realize the value of your teleseminars, you have positioned yourself as someone they can trust and will want to do business with.

Webinars

A *webinar*, also referred to as a webcast, *online event*, or *web seminar*, is similar to a teleseminar in many respects, but it is broadcast to a select group of individuals through their computers via the Internet.

A webinar allows the speaker to share PowerPoint presentations, videos, web pages, and other multimedia content with audiences that can be located anywhere. They typically include audio and visual components. Visual components are shared through a web-conferencing tool or Internet browser. Audio components are usually broadcast through the audience's computers (through speakers and media players), by telephone, or via services like Skype™.

A webinar also allows the speaker to interact with their audience. Members of the audience can ask the speaker or moderator questions in real time through an instant messaging tool or email.

The benefits of a webinar are higher perceived value, the visual aspects, and that they can be extremely interactive. The challenges are higher costs, increased risk of something going wrong with the technology, and slow computer speeds for some participants. Based on your market, your goals, and your budget, you can decide whether a teleseminar or a webinar is the best choice. The more visual your presentation, the more likely a webinar would be your best choice. Other considerations are costs, whether to include graphic design work on your presentation material, service provider fees, and if your end users are set up in a way they can watch the event. There are some people who are still on dial-up service, which prohibits their flexibility for many online offerings.

Regardless of whether you choose teleseminars, webinars, or both, you are able to more fully position your message through this type of training venue. They position you as an expert. The more you are perceived as an expert, the more you are the go-to person whom many people will seek out.

Chapter 15

Aligned Joint-Venture and Affiliate Partnerships

On our own, there is only so much we can do to reach our market. When we join with others who have a similar market reach, we are able to accomplish much more. Enter joint-venture partnerships.

A *joint-venture partnership*, or JV for short, is an agreement between two or more people in which everyone benefits in some way. The primary purpose is cross promotion, with one partner selling a product while increasing market reach and subscribers for all partners.

One of the most common JV arrangements in online marketing is when a partner agrees to send out a message to their market about a specific campaign that another partner is promoting.

Over the years I have increased my opt-in subscriber list by thousands through online JVs. As my business has grown into a more socially conscious one, I seek out aligned partnerships rather than simply partnering with someone to make money. It's about serving the market.

You have likely seen JVs used for book launches. On a specific day an author sells their book via Amazon. A partner agrees to send a message to their market about the book. In return for promoting book, the author offers some type of incentive to those who purchase the book through the partner. It can be a free item or a discount on an item; ideally, the incentive is free. It can be an ebook, report, audio, etc.

Assume you are spearheading just such a partnership. Let's say you secure ten partners who each have a market reach of 1,000 people, and you have a market reach of 1,000 people. Your market reach has gone from 1,000 people seeing your message to 11,000 people seeing it.

Although these types of campaigns can work in markets that have not been saturated by book launches, in many markets blasting out messages about a book on a particular day in order to make a splashy impact doesn't work like it used to because so many of us are experiencing information overload. More is not the key. Quality is.

An essential element of success for JVs is for everyone involved to do what they agree to do. With a well-organized partnership in which everyone follows through, you can reap incredible benefits:

➡ Substantially increase your opt-in subscriber list
➡ Increase visibility on the Internet
➡ Reach more of your target market
➡ Increase traffic to your website, blog, or landing page
➡ Create future opportunities to sell your product to those who download your incentive
➡ Participate in a one-of-a-kind campaign

The Power of Aligned Partnerships

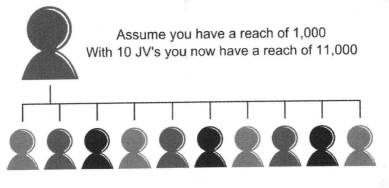

Assume you have a reach of 1,000
With 10 JV's you now have a reach of 11,000

Choose Your Partners Wisely

In a perfect world, JVs would be hassle free. In reality, there are areas of consideration, such as:

➡ What are the reputations of your potential partners?
➡ Will they follow through?
➡ What is the quality of the incentives they are offering?
➡ Is the market you are targeting oversaturated with JVs and the offers they are making?

JVs Are Par for the Course

There are lots of people who make JVs a standard aspect of doing business. In one of the first JV campaigns I spearheaded well over a decade ago, we sold over $15,000 of a $37 product. After affiliate commissions, I made over $7,000 by bringing on joint-venture partners. I set it up to be a win/win for everyone in that the partners could also become affiliates for the campaign. Not only did hundreds of new people opt in in order to get the expert's ethical bribe, but when a customer used the affiliate's link to order my product, the partner/affiliate received 45 percent of the sales price. It's no wonder that JVs have been a major cornerstone for the success of my business.

Joint-venture partnerships are simply strategic alliances. They allow you to enter into a partnership that increases your and your partner's opportunities to reach a larger target market and increase profits. In essence you are leveraging one another's market position. You can promote many different products using this approach.

I managed a very elaborate JV campaign that was essential in achieving the goal of our book, *The Law of Achievement*, becoming an Amazon.com bestseller. Without the support, commitment, and follow-through of our JV partners, the campaign would not have been anywhere near as successful as it was. Because we had everything in place, we actually sold more books on May 2, 2006, than *The DaVinci Code*, *The World is Flat*, and *Freakonomics*. On that day we sold over $23,000 worth of books, our partners substantially increased their opt-in subscriber lists, and those who purchased the book received incredible value.

You can use JV campaigns and partners to promote teleseminars, books, e-reports, ebooks, MP3s, live events, and virtually anything you sell. As previously mentioned, when your partners are also affiliates, they share in the profits. You can also use JVs just to increase your opt-in lists and the lists of your partners, and bring incredible value to those who opt in for the incentives – without selling anything.

Finding Joint-Venture Partners

You can find partners in a number of ways, including through your current customer base, your competitors, and forums. Here are some more:

- Brokers
- Online through newsletters you receive from people you know and trust
- Other campaigns
- Sites that seem like a good match for your market

Again, be sure your partners are reputable. You can do more harm than good if you partner with unscrupulous people. In a couple of embarrassing situations a partner of mine agreed to provide a certain incentive but when it came time for someone to download the incentive, they were taken to a sales page. I blacklisted that partner. Online communities are interesting in that they can be massive, yet in many ways are very small. Experts do talk to each other and share stories about disreputable partners.

Affiliate Partnerships

One of the best ways to provide excellent resources to your market or tap in to other markets with your products is with an *affiliate partnership*. In this type of partnership, your affiliate partner helps sell your product or service by marketing to their customers, and receives a percentage of that sale based on performance. If you have products to sell and you want a greater market reach with increased revenue-generating opportunities, others can be your affiliates.

Common items to sell through an affiliate are software programs, e-products, and seminar registrations. This type of partnership allows for increased revenue streams while providing added value for existing clients by offering products that are beneficial to them.

One challenge with online affiliate partnerships is the inexperienced marketer who encourages people to buy something they themselves have not tried and know nothing about – basically trying to make a quick buck. For an affiliate partnership to be most effective, research what is being promoted and only offer items that are good matches for the market being targeted.

Considerations in choosing affiliate partnerships are:
➼ How credible is the product or service?
➼ How long has it been on the market?
➼ Is the market saturated with other people selling the item?
➼ Is there a large enough market?
➼ What is your percentage of the sale?
➼ How and when are payments made?
➼ What is the reputation of the person you will be selling the product for?

Most who seek out partners get turned down more often than they hear the coveted words "Yes! I would love to promote for you." There are very good reasons why this is so. It's not because these people don't want to partner, it's because what they are being asked to market is not a great fit for them at that particular time.

During a recent two-week period I had no fewer than ten requests to promote products as an affiliate. Some offered an affiliate commission while others made the request simply because "you have a good list." I turned down all but one request. Here's why: Every single one wanted me to promote either that day or within a few days of their request. The one I accepted was from a trusted friend and colleague. I was familiar with the product he asked me to promote and what he offered was a great fit for my market. The price point was low enough that I didn't need to prepare promotions other than to let my community know about the offer. Another reason was that his commission structure was very generous. Even though I knew the other potential partners from my social networks and they were likely on my subscriber list, I turned them down for one (or more) of the following reasons:

- What they wanted me to promote was not a good fit with what my market expects from me.
- The time frame was way too short.
- Commissions were poor or nonexistent – not that I have to get compensated for everything I promote, but if commissions are not in line with what is standard, I likely won't find it appealing enough.
- I was not familiar with the product they wanted me to promote.
- I didn't want to further overload those on my list with emails.
- The price point was incredibly high and too much of a risk for a first-time partnership.
- I plan campaigns as much as six months in advance, the average being at least two to three months.
- Not one person whom I had not yet worked with offered me their product to preview. When someone approaches me they must be willing to let me review the full product. It's different if I approach someone to promote their product; in that case I should be willing to purchase it.

I'm sure some of those I turned down were frustrated by my response, but my primary concern is for the well-being of my subscribers above and beyond anything else. Wondering how other experts feel about these requests, I asked some of my closest friends to weigh in on them:

David Perdew, Niche Affiliate Marketing System Founder

Yesterday I finished my most successful online promotion, and the five-day sale was conceived and executed within twenty-four hours. Although profitable, it was a huge mistake to wait until the last minute because I probably could have done ten times as much business if I had planned four weeks in advance. These are the attributes that made my last-minute promotion successful:

➡ The value was through the roof. It was the kind of value and price that made people think, "Holy cow, how fast can I promote this and how often!"

➡ I didn't think about approaching people to promote this for me if we didn't already have a substantial business relationship.

➡ If my top affiliate partners brought in some of their best affiliate partners, **they got a referral bonus.**

➡ I made sure affiliates expended zero effort by providing all the link, login, and promotion tools they needed to be successful.

➡ I took no for an answer. Because my affiliate referrals are tagged automatically in the database tagging system, many of the affiliates were already making sales on the promotion from the prospects they had driven into the pipeline previously. If partners couldn't promote, **I promoted for them.**

➡ Relationships matter. If I don't have one, I need to make that happen first.

SIDENOTE – David's was the one campaign I immediately said yes to. I know, like, and trust David, we have worked on several campaigns together, and what David was offering was a great fit for my market.

Denise Wakeman, Boost Your Visibility

While it may be tempting to reach out to the influencers in your niche to promote your launch, without a prior relationship, the answer is most likely going to be no. Before you send that request, ask yourself the following questions:

➤ Has there been any previous communication between you and the potential high-profile JV partner?
➤ What have you done for the prospective JV partner lately?
➤ Have you promoted the JV prospect's products or services?
➤ Do you read and comment on the prospect's blog?
➤ Do you actively contribute to the prospect's social networks? Are you retweeting their tweets, sharing their blog posts, and commenting on their Facebook page?
➤ Have you purchased any of the prospect's products?

If the answer is yes to any of the above, then how are you going to make this a win-win for your JV partner?

How much lead time are you giving your JV partner? Most high-profile marketers require a long lead time, as their own promotions and other JV promotions are scheduled months in advance. Three days' notice doesn't cut it.

Most important, do your research. Is your product a good fit for their audience? Have you provided access to your product so they can see for themselves if it's relevant for their audience?

Don't be offended if they say no. There're a lot of factors that go into a decision whether to promote or not. First and foremost there needs to be a relationship established and you can get attention by giving without asking for anything in return. That will get attention.

Ellen Britt, The Future of Ink

I totally agree with all of the really excellent questions that Denise Wakeman suggests you ask yourself before approaching an influencer in your niche. Certainly you should do as many of the things listed as you possibly can AND if it is at all feasible, make it a priority to actually meet the influencer in your niche in person by going to a conference they are going to attend.

Most influencers will let their subscribers and social media followers know about any upcoming events they are attending. Often they will be promoting that event. If this is the case, purchase your event ticket through their affiliate link. If they are presenting at the event, make sure you attend their presentation.

Ask thoughtful questions during the Q&A time that add to the value of the material being presented. Afterwards, take a few minutes and introduce yourself to them, referencing any communication or promotion you have done for them in the past.

Ask them if they are open to a ten-minute conversation during one of the breaks about possibly being a partner in your launch. They still may not say yes to your launch invitation, but you will have made an indelible impression on them by going out of your way to meet them in person. Avoid asking them if they will have lunch or dinner with you. Most influencers' event schedules are completely packed with meetings and pre-arranged get-togethers with clients and colleagues.

Susan Lassiter-Lyons, www.SusanLassiterLyons.com

JV partners are one of the best ways I know of to spread your message. When approaching potential JVs, here's a tip that's always worked for me: Make sure you are offering value first and be prepared to build and nurture the relationship.

Most JVs have marketing calendars that are planned way in advance, but they are always looking for ways to make their promotions better.

Be sure to share recent results that other well-known JVs have gotten promoting your programs, especially EPC (earnings per click).

Sharing *best-practice* or other creative promotional strategies in your niche will go a long way in establishing credibility and that relationship. Then, when they do promote be sure to pay on time and do something special around the holidays. We always send our top ten affiliates a bottle of Dom Perignon or Cristal for Christmas, and we usually get on the calendar with no problem!

Partnerships are definitely a great way to serve your market. Based on what my four colleagues have shared, is it time for you to revisit the way you approach potential partners? If so, now's the perfect time.

A Winning Combination

Affiliate and joint-venture campaigns are some of the best business ventures around, but they might not be a good fit for your particular business. Take into account your own online and marketing strategies. Like any other relationship, online partnerships take time to develop, and you have to put effort into maintaining them and deal with a variety of personalities. By doing your homework you can determine if it's a good fit for your business model.

Chapter 16

Expert Interviews for Reach, Credibility, and Product

As you position your expertise, you increase your opportunities on many levels, and other experts become extremely willing to work with you.

Working with experts is a great way to gain instant credibility, penetrate a large market, and generate revenues. It's actually much easier than most people realize to find experts who are willing to be interviewed for your teleseminar or information product, if you position the opportunity as a win/win for all parties involved.

You can interview an expert by phone or by sending them a series of questions in a Word document. You can interview a single expert or find several who will complement one another and bring extremely high value to your market.

If you are going to do a phone interview, it is important to be fully prepared in order not to take up more of the expert's time than necessary. If you are not comfortable conducting a live interview, record the call and have it transcribed and edited for a higher-quality end product. If you are extremely new to interviewing others, you may need to invest in coaching or training in effective interviewing skills. An investment of time and money in this type of coaching can be invaluable.

Who to Interview

Interview anyone your market is interested in learning from. You can survey your market to find out who those people are. Put together an "expert wish list." When you have three to twelve experts on your list, begin to contact them.

Experts Abound

Virtually any industry has experts who would be happy to be interviewed. Considerations should be:
➼ Who has something to offer your market?
➼ Who can you share markets with?
➼ Who would be willing to let you use the material for a product?

Finding Experts

There are countless places to find experts. They can be as close as your own backyard. Start here:

➻ Your own circle of influence
➻ Your social networks
➻ Forums
➻ Web search

A great way to find experts to partner with is at conferences. Whether you approach the coordinator, a speaker, or an attendee, nothing can compare with this kind of networking. However, it's absolutely essential to respect their time and space. It can be very frustrating for a speaker to be approached by countless individuals who "just want five minutes of your time to pass an idea by" during a conference. The best approach is to introduce yourself, get the other person's card, and contact them after the event if they appear to be pressed for time. You are likely to get much farther this way.

Be Prepared

Before you approach an expert with your idea or proposal, be very clear about what you will be asking of them. Nothing can make an opportunity sour faster than not being organized. Quickly and professionally convey:

➻ Why you want to interview them
➻ What the benefit is to them
➻ What their role will be
➻ What your expectations are as far as time commitments, help with marketing, and promoting to the expert's own market.

Don't be demanding or the expert will most certainly not work with you. In many cases they will not help with marketing. They are often approached by people whose main objective is to secure marketing support from them, which is not a win/win proposition. Be aware of this and treat them respectfully.

Clearly Communicate the Benefits

Be sure the expert can realize a true benefit from working with you. If your expert makes tens of thousands or hundreds of thousands of dollars a month, and you tell them they can make a couple hundred dollars or gain lots of visibility through your subscriber list, they might not view the opportunity as beneficial. They might actually be more interested in helping you if you tell them you are just starting out, and you are upfront and honest about it. Be sincere and professional, and follow up with integrity.

Here's Proof:

244

My client Dr. Joe Capista had the opportunity to interview the author of the *E-Myth* series of books, Michael Gerber, as well as many other experts. Before approaching the experts, we very strategically did everything as outlined on the previous pages, and the resulting product showcased above was superb. We made it very easy for the experts to say yes.

If you know the expert personally, often all it will take is a phone call or email without a lot of detail to get an interview with them. Depending on how involved the project will be, you might want to enter into a contract, or your expert might request one.

To Pay or Not to Pay Experts

There's no hard and fast rule about paying an expert for an interview. In many cases they prefer either a percentage of what you earn on your product or to sell something of their own through your product. Or you may be able to be their affiliate if you set up the interview and arrange for the marketing and distribution. If they are well-known in their industry and have a hot product, you can easily make several hundred to several thousand dollars through an affiliate arrangement; that is, if you have your systems in place.

Some experts prefer to be paid a flat fee. In that case, if you can repackage the interview and sell it, that will allow you to recoup your investment.

Repurposing Interview Content

It's one thing to interview someone and something completely different to get the word out about it. An expert interview is a great opportunity to repurpose information in these ways:

- Sell recordings of the interview.
- Sell transcripts of the interview.
- Be an affiliate seller of your guest's material.
- Sell e-reports written from the transcript.

You can develop a free or for-sale product from the interview. Base your decision on your overall goals. If you have a relatively small opt-in list, a free offer can increase the size of your list.

If you plan on selling any of these products, make sure the expert knows about it. You can add it to your written agreement. You can offer your guest a high percentage of whatever you make from these information products. If they will draw a large number of buyers, this is a great option. Keep in mind that you will need to market the products.

There is really no limit to repurposing an expert interview. It's a matter of how creative you are willing to get.

Host an Expert Series

Another option is to create an "expert series" in which you interview anywhere from six to twelve experts and package the interviews in a bundle. An expert series is one of the fastest ways to gain visibility and market reach. However, as has been mentioned, you absolutely must be prepared before you present your ideas to the experts.

One of the most common types of expert series is a telesummit. A telesummit is a virtual online conference that offers a lineup of a variety of speakers over a few days or several weeks.

There are other types of expert series such as hosting one expert a week on a teleseminar or webinar for a specified or indefinite period of time. Over a period of time you build a following with those who have an interest in the speakers you host.

One of the main reasons to host an expert series, regardless of the format, is to position your own status as an expert. Many an unknown person became quickly well-known due to bringing top experts to their market through an expert series. You build relationships with top people who can catapult you to a very visible position. When you share the virtual stage with leading experts, it is assumed you, too, are a leading expert.

Be sure to put ample time into planning your event. This is not the time to cut corners. You should determine:

➤ When your expert series will take place
➤ How many speakers you will invite
➤ The time frame in which the event will happen
➤ Cost-free or fee?
➤ The registration process
➤ Whether or not you will have learning guides
➤ Whether to allow time for questions and answers

From there get the commitments from your experts. It's essential to line up experts your market wants to hear from. There's no point in bringing on speakers whom others have no interest in. You also want to make sure your speakers are engaging and can captivate the audience with their presentations.

Once you have everything in place, promote your event. This is where JV partnerships and affiliate partnerships can benefit the outcome of your event. The more you can get the experts involved in the process of promotions, the better.

Hosting a telesummit requires a lot of work; there are a lot of details that go into creating a successful event. But when done right it can be a great way to position your expertise, build your opt-in list, and generate revenue while serving your market.

Several of my clients have put their online business on the map by hosting an expert series. One client built her list by nearly 5,000 and grossed $35,000 in revenue. A colleague of mine built her list by over 11,000 with a well-planned and executed expert series.

There's no reason you can't benefit from hosting your own telesummit or weekly expert series. The only way to find out is to do it.

Chapter 17

Lights! Camera! Action! Video to Position Your Message

Video for Marketing and Credibility

Has the thought of being in the movies ever appealed to you? Dreamed of having your own television show? Want to be seen by hundreds, thousands, and even millions of viewers? If you said yes, then video is for you.

Video is one of the hottest marketing tools around. Not only is it great for promotions, but when done right, viewers really feel that they've gotten to know you, and that translates to great marketing.

There are two basic approaches to video: direct to camera and screen capture. *Direct to camera* is filming yourself, colleagues, and/or experts conducting a training session, demonstration, or presentation; doing an interview, book trailer, or testimonial; or delivering a speech. You can film your expert interview or any other kind of interview rather than recording it as an audio. Screen capture is turning something on your computer such as PowerPoint slides or online locations into a video.

The number one online video location is YouTube. There are plenty of others, but YouTube gets so much traffic that posting your video there is a "must-do." It's a video-sharing website where users can upload and share videos. Three former PayPal employees created YouTube in February of 2005.

No matter what you're interested in, there are likely video clips about it online. There are millions of video views per day on YouTube. Shouldn't your video be part of those views? You can use video to gain visibility, promote products, and build your subscriber list. Since YouTube is by far the most popular video site, I focus on YouTube in this chapter. To load videos, do a search on YouTube on "mechanics." Search further on "subscribing to YouTube," "loading a video," and "setting up a You-Tube channel."

The Purpose of Video

The two main uses of YouTube in terms of marketing and your business are to gain visibility and to do research on virtually any topic. It's a great way to connect with your market if you're comfortable in front of a camera. You are viewed as a real person, and people feel more connected to your message than they do using other media.

The more you practice in front of the camera, the easier it is. When you use screen shots, you will record a *voice-over* rather than being on camera. If you are uncomfortable with being on camera or recording your voice, simply have someone else do it. But give it a try before you decide that you truly can't do it – getting your own personality out there is really the point. Focus on the benefit to your market and business, and it should make the task much easier.

What Is Your Message?

Four areas to focus on when doing video are:

➡ Who are you?
➡ Who is the video for?
➡ What problem are you solving?
➡ What is the solution you offer?
➡ When you can clearly answer these questions, your videos will be more beneficial to your viewers.

Your Own Channel

One of the best things about YouTube is that you can create your own *channel*, which acts as your home page at YouTube. This allows for enhancing your brand and subscriber list, and it's easy to do by following the directions. Your channel includes your account name, account type, your uploaded videos, and any user information you enter. You'll have a YouTube subscriber list so those on your list can stay on top of the videos you release.

The more people on your subscriber list, the more people who will get your message. And when you have something to promote, you can reach more potential buyers. As with other areas of your online visibility, proactively promote your channel through your Facebook page, Twitter, LinkedIn, and any other social media networks you use. Add your channel address to your sig file or resource box with a bit about what your channel addresses.

SEO with Videos

Videos are one of the best ways to get SEO. Use your keywords in your video title, video description, tags, and the words you speak. Google picks these up and your SEO improves.

Include a clickable URL in the first line of the description tag (the first line is most important). To make your URL a clickable link, be sure to include the "http://www"part of the address. Viewers can then go directly to your website, blog, or landing page. This is what is meant by a clickable URL: Rather than www.PowerUpForProfits.com use http://www.PowerUp-ForProfits.com

When you're promoting an event, book, or product, posting videos on YouTube will result in a higher search-engine ranking, so be sure to include YouTube in your social media marketing mix.

Consistency Is Key

Once you add videos to your marketing strategy, keep up a consistent flow of videos on YouTube, especially when you have subscribers. They subscribed for a reason: to see what you are up to, learn from you, and follow your message.

Types of Videos

➡ Demonstrations
➡ Mini-presentations

252

- Book trailers
- How-tos

How-tos are the best for SEO. Let's say you are a dog trainer. What better use of a video clip than to give a "how-to" demonstration of a training tip? If you're a chef and want to teach viewers how to use a certain type of cooking utensil, what better way than with a video? If you teach a specific art technique, video is definitely the way to go. You can film a short portion of a training session to tease your viewer, then direct them to where they can get the full training information. There are unlimited uses for video.

Ways to Promote Your Video

Once your video is posted, you can tweet the URL, post it to your Facebook wall, and put the actual video in your blog by using the embedded code.

Another way to gain visibility for yourself and your channel is to comment on other people's videos in a related field, industry, or topic. The more you can pinpoint your comments, the better. Many people search out more than one video about their interest, so the more comments you leave, the better. (And the more videos you post that this market would be interested in, the better). Make your comments substantial rather than simply saying "Nice video."

Search out high-traffic videos. You can tell how popular a video is by looking at the number of views. Depending on the topic, viewer interest and a video's relevance determine how many views it gets.

About a year ago I met a gentleman who was averaging well over 100,000 views for each of his videos. They had to do with the sport of boxing. That's a number most people would be very happy with. Unfortunately he had done nothing to drive viewers from his videos to an opt-in opportunity. I advised him to insert a live link at the beginning of the description of each video and add an invitation to request a free report to get them on his subscriber list. From there I recommended he provide high-value information to subscribers to gain trust from this market. Then he could introduce paid products and services. By implementing this one strategy, this gentleman was able to build an opt-in list that he could now offer paid products to.

To make a strategy like this work you must be consistent. To gain viewers with no backend plan is somewhat of a waste. Think in terms of continued value to your market, leading to earnings.

The viral aspect is the great thing about videos. When people like videos, they tweet about them, mention them on their Facebook walls, post links on their blogs, and add them to articles, just to name a few ways videos gain traction. Add to these a way to drive traffic to your subscriber list, and it's a pretty sweet deal.

Other Considerations

Determine your purpose for creating video, what you hope to accomplish, and who would want to watch your video. You'll have better results if you set a clear intention.

Next time you plan to attend a conference, determine who you want to meet and do short interviews with. Most experts are very open to providing short interviews, and by short I mean two to five minutes. Imagine how much value you could provide to your market if you found six or ten experts to interview; your tribe would love it.

Before recording someone else at a conference or other event, be sure you have permission. Some speakers forbid recording other than by their own staff.

Equipment

There are a number of options when it comes to filming equipment. One of the easiest things to use is a computer video cam for recording from your office. Another is your iPhone. There are plenty of inexpensive video cameras on the market that surpass the limitations of these. When I began doing lots of video, I bought a Flip camera for about $100. I used it for well over two years before upgrading to the Kodak Zi8.

Of course there is always the option of shooting in a studio. This is a major investment, so if you're not fully prepared you can waste a lot of time and money. If you plan well you can shoot several videos in a short period of time at a studio and project an extremely professional image.

Granted, you want very high quality for a welcome video on your website or blog. But in most cases you don't need studio-quality video. If it's a simple training video, you don't need Hollywood production quality. What you should strive for is to get quality information to market. Do a YouTube search on loading video from various devices to get specifics about the device you use.

Don't procrastinate about getting videos out to market because you don't have high-end equipment. In many cases it is better to start with what you have and grow from there.

Video is such a great way to quickly build a nice connection with your market that I strongly encourage you to get past any fears you might have about it and give it a try.

Chapter 18

Ten Lessons
I Have Learned

There are leaders and there are followers. Leaders are usually risk takers; they are willing to fail in order to succeed. They are not afraid of hard work, they know success takes effort, and they teach others lessons based on their own trials and errors.

In building my own sustainable online business I've learned a lot of things that come from being willing to stick with it long enough to have made plenty of mistakes, had plenty of successes, and be considered one of the leaders and experts in my industry. The top ten lessons I have learned are:

Lesson 1: People don't always understand until they walk a mile in your shoes.
Someone who has not done product development, Internet marketing, and building a sustainable business cannot understand the full scope of what this entails. There is always more to it than meets the eye.

There are always plenty of people who will give you advice, but be sure you listen to those who have been there, done that. It will be to your benefit.

Lesson 2: Technology is great… to a point. All things have hiccups.
Although we love technology for all it can do, there are definite downsides to it. For example, email is great, but sometimes emails get lost in cyberspace. This is bound to happen when you are marketing and selling online. There will be times, no matter how many checks and balances you have in place, when something isn't delivered. You can do as much as possible to prevent this from happening, but there will still be occasions when you deliver information and it is not received.

Let's say you just launched a new product, and for any number of reasons the all-important welcome message doesn't reach a new buyer. Most people are pretty rational and kind when they inquire about the product they purchased, but occasionally someone immediately accuses you of ripping them off – shorting them an ebook, an MP3, an e-report, or other product. Even if they've been getting your information for a while, it's as if some folks are just waiting for you to slip up. Oh yes, dear reader, there are people who immediately attack rather than sending a message or making a call to let you know they didn't get what they purchased.

The longer you conduct business online, the more likely it is that something will go wrong and cyber-mud will be flung at you. Be patient if someone sends you a snippy message. Once you get a message or two like this, it is much easier to empathize when you don't get something you paid for. Ninety-nine percent of the time a very simple message in response resolves the issue.

Lesson 3: Consistency is essential to one's success.
Success isn't a haphazard event; it is a step-by-step process – some big, some small. When you are taking the steps you may not see immediate results. But as you look back over a period of months you will see some amazing progress – that is, if you have been consistently moving toward your goal of success.

Many people foolishly buy into the "get rich quick" mentality. There are occasions when someone experiences a windfall and mistakenly believes this will always be the case, but a solid foundation is essential, as are daily action steps that move you toward your vision.

Lesson 4: Investing time and money is an absolute in building any business.
Some people think they can buy one ebook, read one or two books, listen to one teleseminar, and presto – they will make money hand over fist. It doesn't work this way. There are investments of time and money that all of us must make.

Some are fixed investments such as subscription fees, automation software that requires a monthly payment, the ongoing services of experts who can do for us what we cannot do for ourselves, and utility bills. There are other investments such as specialized training, coaches or mentors, attending conferences, and services such as design work, editing, postage, and other such things.

Recently I was asked what I consider to be one of my greatest mistakes in business. By far it is not investing in a mentor sooner than I did. I mistakenly believed I couldn't afford a mentor, when I really couldn't afford to be without one. Fast-forward to today, and I now know beyond the shadow of a doubt how important a mentor is. This year alone I am investing more in one mentor than I used to make in a year. Making an investment in a high-priced mentor is not something to be taken lightly, but something you should consider if you are serious about growing your business.

As your business grows, so will your monthly expenses (investments). Before spending money, evaluate how necessary the purchase of a product is. If you have a "gotta have" feeling, think about it for a day or two, and if you still feel the same way, make the purchase. If you have a business partner, set a rule about what amount of money you each need to discuss with the other before spending. This often eliminates impulse purchases that are not necessary.

A great many people buy program after program and do little more than glance at the material. Then they wonder why the information is not working for them. Don't make this mistake. When you are interested in buying a program, invest in a mentor or join a membership program, and commit to applying the information in order to get as much value out of your investment as you possibly can. To not do so is a huge waste of money.

Lesson 5: All work and no play makes you boring, stressed out, lackluster, and not fun to be around.
Yep! I speak from experience. In the first few years of running my business I went overboard on how much time I put into it. I ate, drank, slept, and talked business all the time, to the point at which friends and family told me I needed to get a life.

This is not how my life is today. Now I find time for other things like exercise, family time, hobbies, spiritual development, my pets, and much, much more. A life that is focused solely on business is not a life of true success. Balance is the key.

Lesson 6: If you've had a passion for any length of time, you likely have more information on the topic than you realize.
It's amazing how much information most people already have regarding their passion. After you develop your first product – an ebook, a white paper, or whatever it may be – you will realize you have more where that came from. It's very exciting to see the big aha! on clients' faces when they realize they have a vast knowledge base that can be packaged in a number of different ways.

This is where repurposing is so valuable. You can take information you put into one format and create a completely different format for it. The possibilities are endless. It simply takes focus, vision, belief, and application to see what is really possible.

Lesson 7: Automating is essential to take your business to the next level.
One of the most important lessons I learned very early on is to automate whenever possible. Early on (and I'm going back several years) I sent out my first ezine one message at a time. Arghhh. It could take all day to do what now takes pressing a single button.

The things that are most important to automate are your opt-in subscriber list, shopping cart, product delivery, recurring payments, much of your social-media marketing, and anything that is time-consuming for no good reason other than to save a few dollars.

Not to automate can lose you a considerable amount of time and money. The nice thing is that there are lots of free automation tools available for those on a tight budget. However, as you grow, so should the sophistication of your automation.

Lesson 8: Know when to outsource.

One of the best things I've ever done was to outsource tasks that took too much of my time, I didn't know how to do and didn't have the time to learn, or were repetitive. Solopreneurs often try to do all the tasks of the business themselves. Initially you may have to do a lot of your own work, but set aside a percentage of what you bring in to outsource a little at a time.

As with any investment, think through why you are outsourcing and what the benefit will be. Here's a partial list of what to outsource:

- Article submission
- Bookkeeping
- Design work
- Social media marketing
- Editing and copywriting
- Physical product fulfillment
- Transcription services

Lesson 9: Surround yourself with winners.

Who you hang out with is just as important as what you do day-in and day-out. It's easy to consider yourself successful when you surround yourself with low achievers. The true test is to surround yourself with high achievers. The winners are those who don't let outside factors determine their success. They understand that they need to maintain a positive outlook on what they are doing, and they are willing to pay the price.

Get involved in mastermind groups. If you are in a mastermind group and it is not a productive experience, be willing to find another group. Pay people to mentor you. Ask any successful person if they invest in mentors, coaches, mastermind groups, etc., and the likely answer will be a resounding YES!

Know that you are worth it. But as with anything you invest in, *use* the information you gain.

Lesson 10: You will be called "lucky" when you succeed.

I love this one. "I am an overnight success and it only took me fifteen years to get here." Many a successful entrepreneur will share a similar story about what it took for them to succeed – years of work, dedication, and effort. Yet many outsiders flippantly call them lucky rather than finding out what they did to succeed.

The fact is, the harder you work, the luckier you get. Success is not something that happens through osmosis. It takes time, energy, learning, mentors, investments, and vision. It also takes being able to manage the ups and downs of your emotions. As my good friend Dr. Joe Capista says, "You can have anything in life you want, if you are willing to pay the price."

Are you paying the price?

Chapter 19

To Your Success

Success Is in the Plan

One of the greatest challenges for many small business owners is finding time to do everything that needs to be done. One important key to your success is time management. Often the thing that needs the greatest attention – continuous marketing – keeps getting moved down the list of priorities because other issues demand more *immediate* attention. Making marketing a priority takes commitment.

Success Mindset

A mindset for success does not happen by chance, but rather by choice and focus. Because I often hear from those who are not achieving at the level they dream of, I like to provide insights into some of the sharpest minds and most successful entrepreneurs I know. Most make their living from the Internet, yet a few don't. Regardless of the industry, each knows the importance of mindset.

Success is achieved more often through a particular state of mind rather than particular circumstances. Your mindset determines how you respond or react to any given situation.

Vision, persistence, willingness to take a risk, and the ability to pick yourself up when you fail are all characteristics of a success mindset. Success is achieved moment by moment, day by day. What appears to be overnight success is almost always many small steps that in hindsight appear to be one giant leap.

The success mindset also has to do with the questions you ask. Rather than asking, "Why me?" when something doesn't work out the way you want it to, ask, "What do I need to do to make this work?" Your mind, heart, and soul will give you the answer if you are open and willing to hear.

The First Hour of Your Workday

The first hour of your day is critical to your success. One of the most common and self-defeating things you can do is check your email first thing in the morning. Your intention may be to take a quick look and get on to something else, but what usually happens is you go off in a number of different directions based on what is in your inbox.

A much better choice is to commit the first hour to monetizing your business by working on a product offering, writing a media release or an article, posting to a forum, writing a blog entry, posting a comment to another blog, updating Twitter and Facebook with highly valuable information, or creating a short video to post on YouTube and other video locations.

Write a Daily To-Do List

This is one of the greatest time-savers you can implement. When you write a to-do list, you have less chance of forgetting what needs to be done. Keep a piece of paper or a small tape recorder handy. As you think of things you must accomplish, write them down or record them. About fifteen minutes before ending your work day, organize all the items you wrote or recorded for the following day and prioritize them. The next morning, review your list and determine if the order of importance is still the same. If yes, jump in. If no, make the necessary changes and begin. Don't work on it until it's perfect. Avoid spending too much time on changes or you will waste time. Commit to getting as many things on your list done as possible.

Prioritize

Which activities are most crucial to achieving your goals? Which tasks can you effectively delegate? Determine which ones you must handle, which ones you can delegate, and which ones you can eliminate as unnecessary.

Organize Your Email Process

Unless absolutely necessary or your particular business demands it, resist the temptation to check your email several times a day.

That's like calling the post office throughout the day to see if you got another piece of mail. In most cases, once in the morning and once in the afternoon is often enough.

Delete any emails you can and respond immediately to those requiring a response. If you need to save a message, transfer it to a separate file so you don't have to keep old messages in your inbox; reserve your inbox for new messages only.

Segment Activities

When you review your to-do list, reserve blocks of time for similar activities. If you have several phone calls to make, do them in a block of time. If you know you will be mailing things, mail them all at once rather than making several trips to the post office. When you have errands, plan out the most direct route for taking care of these tasks. If you need to contact joint-venture partners, set aside a block of time and do it all at once. Segmenting your day this way allows you to focus on activities that require similar methods of application all at one time, making you more efficient.

Create Templates Whenever Possible

If you use the same types of documents on a regular basis, such as a newsletter, contract, or media release, you can save an incredible amount of time by developing templates for them.

Avoid Using Work Time for Personal Activities

A great majority of my clients work from home. It's one of the best ways to run a business today. But there's a temptation to mix personal activities and business activities. If you worked at an offsite office you wouldn't be able to run down to the kitchen to wash dishes, take a quick trip to the market, have coffee with a neighbor, wash a load of clothes, or any number of other tasks that distract home-based business owners.

If this is a challenge for you, put a sign up on your door to let family members, neighbors, and friends know that you are working. Treat your workday the way you would if you were working offsite. Don't turn your home-based business into something you do 24/7. Give it your quality attention for a reasonable period of time each day, and then set it aside for your personal life. The more organized you are, the more you will get done during normal workday hours.

Time Management is Key for Financial Productivity

Life can be, and generally is, chaotic for most of us. Add to that running a solopreneur business as a speaker, author, coach, or consultant, and managing both traditional and online communications, and you have a formula for more chaos.

With even the best intentions we can find ourselves getting further and further behind each day. How can you successfully juggle all that you do and remain productive and growth-oriented? The key is *time management.*

The number one factor that affects time management is focusing on the goal: *billable hours* (or making money). Those of us who have been full-time employees (and most of us have) can easily fall into the pattern of going with the flow of the chaos without regard for what our revenue is each hour.

When you run your own business, you don't get that magical paycheck every two weeks. You can make great money – six figures and beyond – but there are important time-management steps to take to reach that goal.

The first step is to make a list of the tasks you do each day. Stick to basic categories like answering the phone, opening mail, writing blog posts, reading forums, tweeting, reading emails, and surfing the web. Assign each category a value as it relates to your revenue, such as *surfing the web = 2%*.

Next, track your time for the next two days and jot down how much time you spend on each category you identified. You can use an online timer such as http://www.online-stopwatch. com/ to help you do this. Or keep track of the time manually on paper to save time switching around on your computer to find a timesheet document. Be 100 percent honest, because fudging the numbers will negatively impact only your own time management assessment, no one else's. After those two days, assign a percentage of time to each of the items on your log.

The next step is to answer these questions based on your log:

➻ **What can I eliminate?** Tweeting or Facebooking every hour is overkill, and those extra tweets and posts are probably not big revenue generators. In a traditional brick-and-mortar business, you *would not* call your customers and prospects every hour with updates. *Limit your tweets and Facebook posts to once a day and focus them on producing revenue.*

➻ **What can I outsource to someone else?** If writing is not your forte, blogs and forum posts are probably dragging you – and your income potential – down. There are talented people who can do this for you. If you're not comfortable turning over the task to someone else, scale back on what you're doing. Although I encourage you to get your information out to market as much as possible, it is also necessary to determine what bogs you down. If writing one blog post takes you hours instead of just a few minutes, reduce your blog posts from seven to three days per week, remembering to include a call to action in every post.

Other tasks you can delegate include article submissions, media releases, design work, technical details, etc.

Being wildly successful is often determined by how honest you are with yourself about time management and how well you delegate. Wasted time is commonly associated with *procrastination* and/or *indecision*. If you find that you spend an inordinate amount of time online believing it will make you money in the long run, do some soul searching and figure out what you might be avoiding or what you might be in conflict about. Just facing your avoidance issues and solving them can resolve your time management issues!

To get full value from your workday, put systems in place such as the following:

➠ Handling paperwork – When paperwork comes across your desk, decide immediately what to do with it rather than creating piles on your desk that quickly become baffling. You will want to throw much of it out right away, so do so. If someone else is more qualified to handle something than you are, send it to them right away. Either file or respond to the rest. If there are several pieces you must respond to, put them in a folder labeled "awaiting responses" and do them all at once during the block of time you have designated for that task.

➠ Color-coding – You can save a substantial amount of time by assigning specific colors to specific categories in your file system. Rather than searching through dozens or hundreds of manila-colored folders to find something, you have only a few to look at based on the color of the category. For example, put all financial information in green folders, urgent customer issues in red folders, and travel information in yellow folders.

➠ Effective filing – Don't let your filing pile up. If you have to search through stacks of papers when you, a customer, or a colleague needs something, you are wasting your precious time and theirs. When everything is filed in an organized fashion, you can find what you need within moments.

Organizing your time is a choice. But the more organized you are, the more you get done and the more revenue you're likely to produce. And isn't that one of the reasons you run a business? It takes time to develop good time-management and organizational skills, but once you do you will be amazed at how much you can accomplish in any given day.

Chapter 20

Common Terminology

The more you get involved in using the Internet to market and build your business, the more phrases, acronyms, and words you will be exposed to. To make the process as simple as possible, I have compiled a list of many of these common terms. It's by no means a complete list, but includes terms specific to building an online business.

Above the Fold – This is the part of a webpage you see on your screen without scrolling down or over. This is what is considered "prime real estate," in that often visitors make a decision about whether to stay on your page or move on based on what is above the fold. In the context of newspapers it means above the center fold of a newspaper. "Above the scroll" is another phrase that means the same thing.

Add – Noun and verb used on social networking sites to indicate you have added someone to your network. This term has become very popular with the onslaught of social networks.

Affiliate Marketing – A type of Internet marketing in which you partner with other websites, individuals, or companies to send traffic to your site. You can be an affiliate to promote products and services to your market. Others can be your affiliates and market your products and services to their markets. The standard is to get "paid on performance"; in other words, you are paid only when something is sold. Percentages vary depending on the product or service.

Avatar – A graphic representation of a user in a virtual world; it is a character that you can personalize and use when interacting with friends online. Often you can customize an avatar by changing hairstyles, clothes, accessories, and backgrounds. This allows you to create your own unique persona.

Backlinks – Incoming links to a website or webpage. A few of the many ways to get backlinks are to submit the link to directories such as blog and/or Web directories, link exchange with related sites, in your resource box at the end of an article, and through people syndicating your content through RSS feeds.

In basic link terminology, a backlink is any link from another website received by a webpage, directory, website, or top-level domain.

Backlinks are also known as incoming links, inbound links, inlinks, and inward links.

Banned – This happens when pages are removed from a search engine's index specifically because the search engine has deemed them to be violating their guidelines.

You can also be banned from social networks, forums, and other online locations. You can be banned for a short period of time or indefinitely. With social networks the best way to avoid this is to make sure you read the forum rules and guidelines.

Banners and Banner Ads – These small rectangular or square advertisements appear on all sorts of webpages and vary considerably in appearance and subject matter, but they all share a basic function: if you click on them, your Internet browser will take you to the advertiser's website.

Banner ads are usually relatively simple pieces of HTML code, but their presence on the web and their importance in Internet-based business is immense. In simple terms they are picture advertisements. Depending upon their size and shape, banner ads can also be referred to as buttons, inlines, leaderboards, skyscrapers, and other terms.

Banner ads can be static pictures, animated, or interactive. They can appear anywhere on a site. Often, the better the position, the higher the price for posting a banner ad.

Many Web surfers regard these advertisements as highly annoying because they distract from a webpage's actual content or waste bandwidth. However, in other cases, a well-positioned banner ad can work wonders for sales.

Blocking – This is a term that can refer to your own email service or to social networks you belong to. If you are receiving spam in your inbox, with most service providers you can choose to permanently block these messages.

In many social networks you have a choice as to whether or not someone can send you information. Check the rules and regulations of the social networks you belong to.

Blog – A blog (or Web log) is a website where entries are commonly displayed in reverse chronological order. *Blog* can also be used as a verb, meaning *to maintain or add content to a blog*.

Many blogs provide commentary or news on a particular subject; others function as personal online diaries.

A typical blog combines text, images, and links to other blogs, webpages, and other media related to its topic. The ability for readers to leave comments in an interactive format is an important part of many blogs.

Most blogs are primarily textual, although some focus on art, photographs (photoblog), videos, music (MP3 blog), and audios (podcasting), and are part of a wider network of social media.

Micro-blogging is another type of blogging that consists of blogs with very short posts.

Click-Through Rate (CTR) – Click-through rate is a common Internet marketing measurement tool for ad effectiveness. It is the average number of click-throughs per hundred ad impressions, expressed as a percentage.

The CTR measures what percentage of people clicked on an ad to arrive at the intended site; it does not include the people who failed to click yet arrived at the site later as a result of seeing the ad. It tells you how many times people are actually clicking on your ad out of the number of times your ad is shown.

A CTR is obtained by dividing the "number of users who clicked on an ad" on a webpage by the "number of times the ad was delivered" (impressions). For example, if a banner ad was delivered 100 times (impressions delivered) and one person clicked on it (clicks recorded), then the resulting CTR would be 1 percent.

Low click-through rates can be caused by a number of factors including copy, placement, and relevance. Testing various aspects of an ad can help determine how to increase your CTR.

Conversion Rate – In Internet marketing, conversion rate is the ratio of visitors who convert casual content views or website visits into desired actions based on subtle or direct requests from marketers, advertisers, and content creators. The definition of "conversion" depends upon your goals and measurements.

If you are building an opt-in list, conversion could be the ratio of click-throughs to those who opted in. If you are running an ad, it is again the ratio of people who click on the ad to those who purchase. If you are running a survey, it is the ratio of people who clicked on the survey link to those who actually completed the survey.

Cookie – A cookie is a text-only string that gets entered into the memory of your browser. The string is saved to file for future reference. Cookies also provide direct benefits to surfers, including remembering passwords.

> **Getting rid of cookies** – If you are using Internet Explorer, click on the "Tools" menu item at the top of the screen. On the menu that appears, click on "Internet Options." On the "General" tab, there should be an area titled "Internet History" with a "Delete" button and a "Settings" button. Click on the "Delete" button and click on the "Delete Cookies" button on the next screen.

Cost Per Acquisition (CPA) – An online advertising cost structure in which you pay per an agreed-upon actionable event such as a lead, form submission, registration, or sale linked to the advertisement.

Cost Per Click (CPC) – A common way to pay for search engine and other types of online advertising, CPC means you pay a pre-determined amount each time someone clicks on your advertisement to visit your site. You usually set a maximum amount you are willing to pay per click for each search term, and the amount you pay is equal to or less than that amount depending on the particular search engine and your competitors' bids. CPC is also referred to as Pay Per Click (PPC).

Cost Per Impression (CPM) – A common Internet marketing cost structure, especially for banner advertising. You agree to pay a set cost for every 1,000 impressions your ad receives.

Crawler – A Web crawler is a program that browses the World Wide Web in a methodical and automated manner. It also known as a Web spider, Web robot, ant, bot, worm, and automated indexer. Famous examples of Web crawlers are search engines. They make copies of those pages and store them in a search engine's index.

Database Marketing – A powerful competitive tool for building trust and name recognition in your market. In terms of Internet marketing, it has to do with marketing to an opt-in subscriber list.

Directories – A type of search engine that gathers listings through human efforts rather than through Web crawling. In directories, websites are often reviewed, summarized to a brief description, and placed in a relevant category. Some of the most common types of directories are Web, blog, and article directories.

Domain Name – A website's main address.

Ebook – An ebook is an electronic book, one you read digitally on your computer, laptop screen, or devices called ebook readers. An ebook can be the electronic version of a hard copy book. It can also be an information product that has never been in hard copy version.

Ecommerce – The ability to purchase online. Webpages that allow the buying and selling of products or services are commonly called shopping carts.

Email Marketing – The promotion of products or services via electronic mail.

Ezine – The term ezine is short for "electronic magazine." "E-zine," "eZine," and "e-Zine" are spelling variations. A similar term is "ejournal."

Facebooking – Any act of using features on Facebook.

Facebook Friends – Those people you give permission to be in your Facebook network.

Forum – A place on the Internet where people with common interests or backgrounds come together to find information and discuss topics.

HTML – HyperText Markup Language, the programming language used in websites. Developers use other languages that can be read and understood by HTML to expand what they can do on the Web.

Hyperlink – Often blue and underlined, hyperlinks – commonly called "links" for short – allow you to navigate to other pages on the Web with a simple click of your mouse.

Keywords – Words that people use to search for specific topics on the Internet. Keywords can be purchased from search engine companies so that an appropriate banner ad can be displayed when a viewer searches on a particular word.

Landing Page – This is the first page a person sees when they click on an ad or listing. Landing pages are also known as lead capture pages. Almost anytime you direct someone to your website from an advertisement, you should send them to a specialized landing page with targeted information to increase your conversion rate.

Link Popularity – This is determined by how many websites link to yours, how popular those linking sites are, and how much their content relates to yours. Link popularity is an important part of search engine optimization (SEO).

Local Search – A huge and growing portion of the search engine marketing industry, local search allows users to find businesses and websites in a specific (local) geographic area. This includes local search features on search engines and online yellow page sites. Using the correct keywords in the copy makes local searches easier for the user.

Long Tail Keywords – Rather than targeting the most common keywords in your industry, you can focus on niche terms (long tail keywords) that are usually longer phrases but are also easier and quicker to rank in search engines.

Lurk-in Forums – Lurking allows users to learn the conventions of an online community before they actively participate, improving their socialization when they eventually de-lurk.

Meta Search Engine – A search engine that gets listings from two or more other search engines rather than crawling the Web itself.

Meta Tags (see also keyword tags, tags, etc.) – Meta tags allow you to highlight important keywords related to your site in a way that matters to search engines, but that your site visitors usually do not see. Although not as important as they used to be, they still play a key role in SEO.

Natural Listings – These are more commonly referred to as organic listings or organic results. These are non-advertised results, and there is usually no cost to get natural listings. However, some search engines charge a fee.

Niche Market – A narrowly defined group of potential customers/clients. A niche market usually evolves based on market demand for a product or service. Niche markets can arise based on changes in society, technology, or general environment.

Product and service development for a niche market is the process of finding and serving pockets of customers in a profitable way by designing custom-made products and services for the specified market. Niche markets can be very profitable even though they can be small due to specialization. Often large businesses ignore niche markets due to their perception that they have little potential, yet smaller businesses can gain great profit potential by focusing on niche markets.

With the advent of technology there is more opportunity for smaller businesses to optimize their positions by focusing on niche markets.

Opt-in – This type of registration requires a person submitting information to specifically request that they be contacted or added to a list. Opt-ins are usually gathered by way of a form on a website, blog, or landing page.

Opt-out – Someone choosing to get off an opt-in list is opting out.

Outbound Links – Links on a webpage leading to another webpage, whether on the same site or another site. You can have the links open in a new browser window.

Those who oppose outbound linking believe you lose time and money from visitors to your site. Those who like outbound links say they can actually enhance the value of a site and increase the chance of a return visitor.

Paid Listings – Listings that search engines sell to advertisers, usually through paid placement or paid inclusion programs. This is the opposite of organic or natural listings, which are not sold.

Pay Per Click (PPC) – The most common type of search engine advertising cost structure is PPC search engine marketing. Google, Yahoo, MSN, and many more search engines all use PPC. It is an advertising model in which advertisers pay for click-throughs to their websites.

Permalink – A permalink is a URL that points to a specific blog entry after it has passed from the front page to the archives. When referring people to a blog posting you have done, rather than simply giving them your blog address, give them the permalink. This will take them directly to the posting.

Permission Marketing – When someone opts in to your database, they are giving you permission to send them more information. Conversion rates tend to be higher when using permission marketing.

Pop-Under – A pop-under is a small window that opens in a new Web browser window once you visit a particular page or take some other action. They are considered less annoying than pop-up ads because the new window appears behind the existing one.

Pop-Up Ad (or "Pop-up") – An ad that displays in a new browser window. Many people do not like pop-ups, saying they are annoying. This is why pop-unders can be much more effective. Some search engines ban ads that create a certain number (or even any) pop-up ads. Although both pop-ups and pop-unders can be annoying, they can actually increase conversion rates.

Press Release Optimization – The optimizing of press releases for search engines by use of keywords in the headline and body.

Rank – A number that a search engine assigns to a webpage to determine the order of search results. A webpage with a higher ranking generally appears earlier in the search results. Also known as *position.*

To find out your webpage's rank, you can use Page Rank Checker. This is a free tool for checking Google page ranking of any website page easily and to display your site's PageRank™ value on your webpages. http://www.prchecker.info

Reciprocal Link – A link exchange between two sites. Reciprocal links used to be used quite widely, but no longer. One-way inbound links are much more widely used now.

Real Simple Syndication (RSS) – RSS is a family of Web feed formats used to publish frequently updated content including, but not limited to, blog entries, news headlines, and podcasts. For more information go to http://www.whatisrss.com/

Robot or Bot – A robot is an automated program that accesses a website and traverses through the site by following the links present on the pages. Robots are also referred to as Web crawlers and spiders.

Robots.txt – A file used to keep webpages from being indexed or to tell a search engine which pages you want indexed.

Search Engines – Search engines are places people go to search for things on the Internet such as Google, Yahoo, and MSN

Search. Most search engines provide two ways for websites to appear: Organic (free) and Paid.

Search Engine Marketing (SEM) – All forms of online marketing involving search engines – primarily through *search engine optimization* and *paid search marketing*. Also known as positioning, search engine marketing is the process of making a webpage or website score well in search engine rankings.

Search Engine Optimization (SEO) – This is about making your website search-engine friendly. It's the process of optimizing your website for search engines so it displays near the top of search engine result pages (SRRPs). It can be difficult to do on your own, especially with all the changes occurring on an increasingly frequent basis in regard to SEO.

Search Terms – A search term is a word or group of words that a person types into a search engine to find what they are looking for. Researching what words people use to search with is beneficial in knowing what keywords to use and what long tail keywords to use.

Social Media – A type of online media where information is uploaded primarily through user submission. Many different forms of social media exist including established formats like forums, blogs, video sites, and social networks.

Social Networking – Social networking websites allow users to interact and create or change content on the site.

Spam – Unwanted email. There are other definitions of what spam is, but the most common refers to junk email. There are strict standards and penalties associated with the CAN-SPAM Act.

To a search engine, spam is Web content that the search engine deems to be detrimental to its efforts to deliver relevant, quality search results.

Spider – A noun and a verb, search engines have spiders crawl through all the linked pages of a website to gather information pertinent to including the site in their natural listings. They can also be used to determine the ranking of a site on various search terms.

Stickiness – How often people return to a website. Fresh content, constant updates, news feeds, and exclusive content are all ways to make a site stickier.

Tags (OR description tags) – Tags provide a brief description of your site that search engines can understand. A tag should contain the main keywords of the page it is describing in a short summary. Avoid what is known as keyword stuffing – putting a high percentage of the same keyword throughout your copy.

Target Marketing – Developing a marketing campaign to attract a specific group of people.

Target Market – A specific segment of the market that has been identified as your customers or clients. A target market is distinguished by socioeconomic, demographic, and/or interest characteristics that make those people the most likely customers for your products or services.

Teleseminar – A seminar that takes place over the telephone.

Text Ad – An online advertisement that contains only written copy.

Tracking Code – Information typically included in a Web address that allows an advertiser to track the effectiveness of various aspects of an advertisement.

Tweets – A tweet is a post on Twitter. The act of writing a tweet is called tweeting or twittering. Tweets can be up to 140 characters long, including spaces, and can include URLs and hashtags.

Twitter – A social networking website that allows users to stay up to date on the daily activities of their friends and colleagues. Postings appear real-time. As you post, they show up in your stream.

Twittering – Sending a Twitter message. Past tense is tweet.

URL – Uniform Resource Locator. These are the letters and symbols that make up the address of a specific webpage.

Usability – How easy it is for a user to navigate a website and find the information they are seeking.

USP (Unique Selling Proposition) – A statement that identifies what makes a person, product, or organization different from competitors.

Viral Marketing – A method of Internet marketing that attempts to make advertisements, postings, articles, and virtually anything that can be sent to someone else so interesting that viewers will pass them along to others.

Web Browser – The program you use to access the Internet. Common browsers include Microsoft Internet Explorer (IE), Apple's Safari, and Mozilla Firefox.

Webinar – A combination of the words *Web* and *seminar,* these are virtual seminars that allow people from anywhere in the world to attend by way of an Internet connection. Webinars differ from teleseminars in that participants can see visuals during the seminar rather than simply being on the phone.

White Paper – A white paper is an authoritative report or guide that often addresses issues and how to solve them. They are used to educate readers and are often used in politics and business, and for technical subjects.

Wiki – A user-written, controlled, and edited site. Anyone with Web access can change information appearing on Wikis, which can be about broad or specific topics. The best known example is Wikipedia.

NOTE: For more detail about any definition, do a Google search on the term.

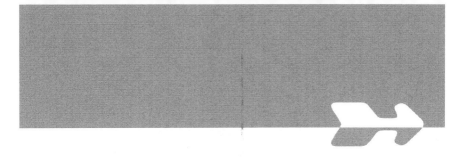

Closing Thoughts

Congratulations! You are among a very small segment of the population by virtue of the fact that you made it to this page. You're reading the conclusion of *Power Up for Profits* for one of two reasons – either you skipped to the end to try to get the message of this book in one fell swoop, or you read the entire book.

If you are among the first group, stop right now and start from page one. You are not going to get the benefit of the information simply by reading the conclusion. There is so much great information contained on the previous pages that you are doing yourself a disservice by not reading it from front to back.

If you have read the entire book, way to go! You are among those who are willing to invest the time and effort to learn all you can to build your business. Building a wildly successful business takes vision, time, effort, investment, planning, and most definitely action. Many people say they want a successful business but are not willing to do what it takes. Something else you must do is take risks. With risks come rewards.

In the spring of 2012, my partner, Karen, and I took a wonderful vacation on the island of Kauai. It was a well-deserved break after the loss of both my parents. It was a time for regrouping emotionally, physically, and spiritually.

We wanted to make this a no-holds-barred trip. Anything we wanted to do, we would do, whether it be to swim with the dolphins, snorkel, take a helicopter ride around the island, enjoy a luau, or eat at the very best restaurants – we would do it.

After checking into the Outrigger Resort we headed on over to talk with the concierge about sights to see. The young man enthusiastically shared dozens of ways we could enjoy our stay. Everything sounded great until we got to ziplining.

Being a daredevil, Karen loved the idea of the zipline experience. As she and the concierge talked about adding this to our list of activities, I could feel my palms become sweaty. This was not my idea of fun. Karen and the young man encouraged me to go for it. In that I had made a commitment to live large and go for new experiences, I sheepishly agreed.

Secretly I prayed that something would happen that would cancel our zipline experience, which just happened to be scheduled for our final full day on the island. On the big day I woke up wondering how I would survive it. You see, I have a fear of heights, and dangling hundreds of feet off the ground by a wire is not my idea of the ideal experience. Realizing my prayer for the experience to be cancelled was not going to happen, I decided to be fully in the experience.

The ride from the resort to the zipline office was filled with Karen excitedly talking about how much fun we would have. If ever I wondered if her idea of fun and mine were different, now there was no doubt. Upon arrival at the welcome area we were asked to sign a waiver. Line by line I read every word on the page. My heart almost pounded out of my chest when I got to the part about the company not being liable in the event of bodily injury or death. Gulp! I asked the other couples who were also signing waivers if they read that line. No one paid much attention to it. Oh my gosh. No attention to injury and death clauses? What was wrong with these people?

After we signed our releases we were led to the training area. Strapping ourselves into harnesses, we were told how to avoid injury and what to expect from the day. Our guides, a young woman and man, were incredibly passionate about what we would experience. Most of us were between the ages of forty and sixty. I found my soul mate in fear when a woman from Texas announced her fear to all of us. I quickly buddied up with her.

We piled into an open-air vehicle that resembled a jeep on steroids. I have to admit, the ten minute ride was exhilarating. Then we were led to the first of nine ziplines. "This is the baby line," Deb, our female guide, enthusiastically shared.

"Baby line?" I thought as I looked at the 212-foot distance from beginning to end of the first line with a drop of about 75 feet. The first person squealed with delight as she zoomed from one end to the other. The second person was equally excited. Then the third. Then me. Deb hooked me up to the wire and told me to just let go.

"Oh shoot!" I thought. "What in the world am I going to do?" It felt as if my shoes were glued to the platform. My palms got sweaty and my face grew flush. "I can't possibly not do this," I reasoned. "If I don't I will ruin the fun for everyone."

I turned to Deb. "How many people have died on this?" She smiled and said, "Zero." I asked her to give me a push. She gladly obliged. The most amazing thing happened. I let go and decided to go with the experience.

"Wow! This is a blast!" I yelled excitedly as I landed on the other side. I had to laugh at myself for being so fearful. The next line was much more fun. And the next and the next and the next. By the time we got to King Kong, I felt like a pro. I was giggling like a schoolgirl who just got asked to the prom. I was ready to conquer King Kong.

There were a few differences with King Kong compared to the others. One, it was the longest of all the ziplines at 1,250 feet. Two, there were two lines side by side, so you went at the same time as your partner. Three, we were given very special instructions: When you get to the end, turn your head and grab the rope.

On the other ziplines the guide on the receiving end helped us stop. On King Kong we had to pull ourselves in by grabbing a special rope. But in order not to knock ourselves out, get a black eye, or lose any teeth, we had to turn our heads to avoid a huge block on the metal line that would help us stop.

"Turn my head and grab the rope. Turn my head and grab the rope. Turn my head and grab the rope," I repeated at least a dozen times. As Karen and I raced to the other side, I repeated, "Turn my head..." I somehow forgot to grab the rope. The last thing I remember before sliding backward was hearing several people yelling, "Grab the rope!"

It didn't take long to realize how absolutely essential all the instructions were. And it didn't take much longer for me to come to a stop midway between the beginning and end of King Kong. In the distance was another group of zipliners who were pointing and saying, "Look! Someone's stranded." To ease my anxiety, I playfully yelled to them, "This could be you!"

I realized that I had a few choices as to what I could do as I hovered hundreds of feet above a cluster of trees and a river. I could panic and make a complete idiot of myself while putting myself in harm's way. I could cry and make a fool out of myself. Or I could let go and "be" with the experience. I chose the latter. Within seconds I found myself actually enjoying the scenery. I thought, "Wow! Talk about attracting that which we most fear. What a lesson."

Although I could see the people in my group doing something with the guide, I wondered why it was taking so long to be rescued. "Yoo-hoo! I'm out here. My legs are going to sleep," I yelled.

"Don't worry, we're sending Bob out to get you," someone yelled.

Bob had to go through a lot of preparation to be able to safely come out over 600 feet to my aid. Finally I saw him grab the metal line and, inch by inch, one hand over the other, make his way out to me. While waiting for Bob, I thought, "This is going to make a great story for a speech or book someday." Boy was I right.

Right before he reached me he told me not to make any quick movements and to put my arms around his shoulders and not let go. Wow! One minute I was letting go and the next I was holding on tight. Slowly we made our way to the platform. Several people were there to pull us in. Once I had my feet planted firmly on the ground, I laughed and said, "That was one of the most incredible experiences I have ever had."

What I learned from my zipline experience is this: Most fear is unfounded. And yet it's our fear that holds us back from living life fully. It is also fear that holds us back in business. Paying attention to the formula that an expert offers – in that case to grab the rope and turn my head – is essential to not screwing up. It's not that we won't mess up on occasion, but we can minimize the frequency. You have been given the formula in *Power Up for Profits* for building your business with proven strategies. You can choose to listen to those who don't have the experience or you can listen to those who do. The choice is yours.

Another very important lesson I learned was to be willing to let go and enjoy the experience and when to hold on tightly. There are times when you can do nothing but let go. It is in the letting go that we allow our Higher Power (Spirit, God, Source, etc.) to give us more than we ever could imagine. Then there are times when we must hold on. This is when persistence comes in.

I also learned that teamwork is essential to an incredible outcome – that is, if you have the right team. The other couples who joined in on the zipline experience when we did were playful, energized, talkative, and loved having a good time. They made the experience what it was. It's the same in your business. If you have the right team, your business can be fun while being successful.

Most of all I learned that life is too short not to go for it. By being willing to walk through my fear and step into the experience, I had a great time, created an incredible memory, and realized I have often shortchanged myself in various areas. So many people do this in their businesses. You will have a fuller life if you commit fully to your business.

I truly believe, as well as know, that our businesses provide for us many things. One, a great living if we are willing to work for it. Two, a lifestyle many only dream of. Three, the ability to serve a community of people who are hungry for a better way of life. With what you have been given in *Power Up for Profits*, you can achieve all of this and more.

I am truly grateful that you took the time to read *Power Up for Profits*. I encourage you to implement the ideas in this book and create a wildly, massively fun and memorable business and lifestyle. After all, there is only one you, and there are people waiting for you to step into your greatness.

Isn't it time?

About Kathleen Gage

Kathleen Gage is the "no-nonsense, common sense" online marketing strategist, speaker, author, product creation specialist, and owner of Power Up For Profits. She helps entrepreneurs make money online. Her clients are driven by making a difference through their own unique voice.

Considered to be one of the nation's most passionate speakers, Kathleen is known for cutting through the fluff and helping people leave their sob stories behind so they can stop focusing on the past and start looking toward the future. She speaks and teaches about what she believes are the core elements of a successful life: accountability, integrity, honesty, and living with passion and hope.

Although Kathleen is recognized as a top leader in her field, this wasn't always the case. She made choices in her teens and early twenties that took her from a comfortable middle-class upbringing to a life of homelessness and being unemployable. She rose above seemingly insurmountable odds to become an award-winning business owner, bestselling author, Internet sales and marketing trainer, and award-winning keynote speaker.

With more than thirty years of experience in sales, marketing, management, public relations, and promotions, Kathleen has consulted with and trained organizations such as the U.S. Marine Corps, Novus Corporation, and AT&T. She has acted in leadership and advisory capacities for many organizations, including being past president of the National Speakers Association Utah Chapter, past vice-chair and marketing chair for the Central Region Council for the Department of Workforce Services of Utah, and a member of the legislative council for the American Cancer Society of Utah.

Kathleen has written dozens of information products and books, has hundreds of interviews to her credit, and is a highly skilled, inspirational keynote speaker. Her mission is to help people understand that their business is merely a means to get their message out to the world. She teaches that it's not just about what you do, but the reasons behind why you do it.

Visit Kathleen's website www.PowerUpForProfits.com to access a special gift on how to you can begin immediately to put her wisdom to work in your business.